A Treatise on the Grace of Christ and on Original Sin

A Treatise on the Grace of Christ and on Original Sin

St. Augustine

A Treatise on the Grace of Christ and on Original Sin

© Lighthouse Publishing 2018

Written by: St. Augustine (Nov.13 354 – Aug.28 430)
Translated by Peter Holmes and Robert Ernest Wallis
Revised by: Professor Benjamin B. Warfield, D.D
Updated into Modern U.S English by A.M. Overett (b. 1960)

All rights reserved. Without limiting the rights under copyright reserved above, no part of this publication may be reproduced, stored in a retrieval system, or transmitted, in any form or by any means (electronic, mechanical, photocopying, recording or otherwise), without the prior written permission of the copyright owner of this book.

Published by
Lighthouse Christian Publishing
SAN 257-4330
5531 Dufferin Drive
Savage, Minnesota, 55378
United States of America

www.lighthousechristianpublishing.com

EXTRACT FROM AUGUSTIN'S "RETRACTATIONS,"

Book II. Chap. 50,

ON THE FOLLOWING TREATISE, "DE GRATIA CHRISTI, ET DE PECCATO ORIGINALI."

"After the conviction and condemnation of the Pelagian heresy with its authors by the bishops of the Church of Rome, —first Innocent, and then Zosimus, —with the co-operation of letters of African councils, I wrote two books against them: one On the Grace of Christ, and the other On Original Sin. The work began with the following words: 'How greatly we rejoice because your bodily, and, above all, because of your Spiritual welfare.'"

A TREATISE ON THE GRACE OF CHRIST, AND ON ORIGINAL SIN, BY AURELIUS AUGUSTIN, BISHOP OF HIPPO; In Two Books, written against Pelagius and Cœlestius in the year a.d.418.

Book I.

ON THE GRACE OF CHRIST.

Wherein he shows that Pelagius is disingenuous in his confession of grace, inasmuch as he places grace either in nature and free will, or in law and teaching; and, moreover, asserts that it is merely the "possibility" (as he calls it) of will and action, and not the will and action itself, which is assisted by divine grace; and that this assisting grace, too, is given by God according to men's merits; whilst he further thinks that they are so assisted for the sole purpose of being able the more easily to fulfil the commandments. Augustin examines those passages of his writings in which he boasted that he had bestowed express commendation on the grace of God, and points out how they can be interpreted as referring to law and teaching,—in other words, to the divine revelation and the example of Christ which are alike included in "the teaching,"—or else to the remission of sins; nor do they afford any evidence whatever that Pelagius really acknowledged Christian grace, in the sense of help rendered for the performance of right action to natural faculty and instruction, by the inspiration of a most glowing and luminous love; and he concludes with a request that Pelagius would seriously listen to Ambrose, whom he is so very fond of quoting, in his excellent eulogy in commendation of the grace of God.

Chapter 1 [I.]—Introductory.

How greatly we rejoice because your bodily, and, above all, your spiritual welfare, my most sincerely attached brethren and beloved of God, Albina, Pinianus, and Melania, we cannot express in words; we therefore leave all this to your own thoughts and belief, in order that we may now rather speak of the matters on which you consulted us. We have, indeed, had to compose these words to the best of the ability which God has vouchsafed to us, while our messenger was in a hurry to be gone, and amidst many occupations, which are much more absorbing to me at Carthage than in any other place whatever.

Chapter 2 [II.]—Suspicious Character of Pelagius' Confession as to the Necessity of Grace for Every Single Act of Ours.

You informed me in your letter, that you had entreated Pelagius to express in writing his condemnation of all that had been alleged against him; and that he had said, in the audience of you all: "I anathematize the man who either thinks or says that the grace of God, whereby 'Christ Jesus came into the world to save sinners,' is not necessary not only for every hour and for every moment, but also for every act of our lives: and those who endeavor to disannul it deserve everlasting punishment." Now, whoever hears these words, and is ignorant of the opinion which he has clearly enough expressed in his books, —not those, indeed, which he declares to have been stolen from him in an incorrect form, nor those which he repudiates, but those even which he mentions in his own letter which he forwarded to Rome, —would certainly suppose that the views he holds are in strict accordance with the truth. But whoever notices what he openly declares in them, cannot fail to regard these statements with suspicion. Because, although he makes that grace of God whereby Christ came into the world to save sinners to consist simply in the remission of sins, he can still accommodate his words to this meaning, by alleging that the necessity of such grace for every hour and for every moment and for every action of our life, comes to this, that while we recollect and keep in mind the forgiveness of our past sins, we sin no more, aided not by any supply of power from without, but by the powers of our own will as it recalls to our mind, in every action we do, what advantage has been conferred upon us by the remission of sins. Then, again, whereas they are accustomed to say that Christ has given us assistance for avoiding sin, in that He has left us an example by living righteously and teaching what is right Himself, they have it in their power here also to accommodate their words, by affirming that this is the necessity of grace to us for every moment and for every action, namely, that we should in all our conversation regard the example of the Lord's conversation. Your own fidelity, however, enables you clearly to perceive how such a profession of opinion as this differs from that true confession of grace which is now the question before us. And yet how easily can it be obscured and disguised by their ambiguous statements!

Chapter 3 [III.]—Grace According to the Pelagians.

But why should we wonder at this? For the same Pelagius, who in the Proceedings of the episcopal synod unhesitatingly condemned those who say "that God's grace and assistance are not given for single acts, but consist in free will, or in law and teaching," upon which points we were apt to think that he had expended all his subterfuges; and who also condemned such as affirm that the grace of God is bestowed in proportion to our merits:—is proved, notwithstanding, to hold, in the books which he has published on the freedom of the will, and which he mentions in the letter he sent to Rome, no other sentiments than those which he seemingly condemned. For that grace and help of God, by which we are assisted in avoiding sin, he places either in nature and free will, or else in the gift of the law and teaching; the result of which of course is this, that whenever God helps a man, He must be supposed to help him to turn away from evil and do good, by revealing to him and teaching him what he ought to do, but not with the additional assistance of His co-operation and inspiration of love, that he may accomplish that which he had discovered it to be his duty to do.

Chapter 4. —Pelagius' System of Faculties.

In his system, he posits and distinguishes three faculties, by which he says God's commandments are fulfilled, —capacity, volition, and action: meaning by "capacity," that by which a man can be righteous; by "volition" that by which he wills to be righteous; by "action," that by which he actually is righteous. The first of these, the capacity, he allows to have been bestowed on us by the Creator of our nature; it is not in our power, and we possess it even against our will. The other two, however, the volition and the action, he asserts to be our own; and he assigns them to us so strictly as to contend that they proceed simply from ourselves. In short, according to his view, God's grace has nothing to do with assisting those two faculties which he will have to be altogether our own, the volition and the action, but that only which is not in our own power and comes to us from God, namely the capacity; as if the faculties which are our own, that is, the volition and the action, have such avail for declining evil and doing good, that they require no divine help, whereas that faculty which we have of God, that is to say, the capacity, is so weak, that it is always assisted by the aid of grace.

Chapter 5 [IV.]—Pelagius' Own Account of the Faculties, Quoted.

Lest, however, it should chance to be said that we either do not correctly understand what he advances, or malevolently pervert to another meaning what he never meant to bear such a sense, I beg of you to consider his own actual words: "We distinguish," says he, "three things, arranging them in a certain graduated order. We put in the first place 'ability;' in the second, 'volition;' and in the third, 'actuality.' The 'ability' we place in our nature, the 'volition' in our will, and the 'actuality' in the effect. The first, that is, the 'ability,' properly belongs to God, who has bestowed it on His creature; the other two, that is, the 'volition' and the 'actuality,' must be referred to man, because they flow forth from the fountain of the will. For his willing, therefore, and doing a good work, the praise belongs to man; or rather both to man, and to God who has bestowed on him the 'capacity' for his will and work, and who evermore by the help of His grace assists even this capacity. That a man can will and effect any good work, comes from God alone. So that this one faculty can exist, even when the other two have no being; but these latter cannot exist without that former one. I am therefore free not to have either a good volition or action; but I am by no means able not to have the capacity of good. This capacity is inherent in me, whether I will or no; nor does nature at any time receive in this point freedom for itself. Now the meaning of all this will be rendered clearer by an example or two. That we can see with our eyes is not of us; but it is our own that we make a good or a bad use of our eyes. So again (that I may, by applying a general case in illustration, embrace all), that we are able to do, say, think, any good thing, comes from Him who has endowed us with this 'ability,' and who also assists this 'ability;' but that we really do a good thing, or speak a good word, or think a good thought, proceeds from our own selves, because we are also able to turn all these into evil. Accordingly,—and this is a point which needs frequent repetition, because of your calumniation of us,—whenever we say that a man can live without sin, we also give praise to God by our acknowledgment of the capacity which we have received from Him, who has bestowed such 'ability' upon us; and there is here no occasion for praising the human agent, since it is God's matter alone that is for the moment treated of; for the question is not about 'willing,' or 'effecting,' but simply and solely about that which may possibly be."

Chapter 6 [V.]—Pelagius and Paul of Different

Opinions.

The whole of this dogma of Pelagius, observe, is carefully expressed in these words, and none other, in the third book of his treatise in defense of the liberty of the will, in which he has taken care to distinguish with so great subtlety these three things,—the "capacity," the "volition," and the "action," that is, the "ability," the "volition," and the "actuality,"—that, whenever we read or hear of his acknowledging the assistance of divine grace in order to our avoidance of evil and accomplishment of good,—whatever he may mean by the said assistance of grace, whether law and the teaching or any other thing,—we are sure of what he says; nor can we run into any mistake by understanding him otherwise than he means. For we cannot help knowing that, according to his belief, it is not our "volition" nor our "action" which is assisted by the divine help, but solely our "capacity" to will and act, which alone of the three, as he affirms, we have of God. As if that faculty were infirm which God Himself placed in our nature; while the other two, which, as he would have it, are our own, are so strong and firm and self-sufficient as to require none of His help! so that He does not help us to will, nor help us to act, but simply helps us to the possibility of willing and acting. The apostle, however, holds the contrary, when he says, "Work out your own salvation with fear and trembling." And that they might be sure that it was not simply in their being able to work (for this they had already received in nature and in teaching), but in their actual working, that they were divinely assisted, the apostle does not say to them, "For it is God that worketh in you to be able," as if they already possessed volition and operation among their own resources, without requiring His assistance in respect of these two; but he says, "For it is God which worketh in you both to will and to perform of His own good pleasure;" or, as the reading runs in other copies, especially the Greek, "both to will and to operate." Consider, now, whether the apostle did not thus long before foresee by the Holy Ghost that there would arise adversaries of the grace of God; and did not therefore declare that God works within us those two very things, even "willing" and "operating," which this man so determined to be our own, as if they were in no wise assisted by the help of divine grace.

Chapter 7 [VI.]—Pelagius Posits God's Aid Only for Our "Capacity."

Let not Pelagius, however, in this way deceive incautious and simple persons, or even himself; for after saying, "Man is therefore to be praised for his willing and doing a good work," he added, as if by way of correcting himself, these words: "Or rather, this praise belongs to man and to God." It was not, however, that he wished to be understood as showing any deference to the sound doctrine, that it is "God which worketh in us both to will and to do," that he thus expressed himself; but it is clear enough, on his own showing, why he added the latter clause, for he immediately subjoins: "Who has bestowed on him the 'capacity' for this very will and work." From his preceding words it is manifest that he places this capacity in our nature. Lest he should seem, however, to have said nothing about grace, he added these words: "And who evermore, by the help of His grace, assists this very capacity,"— "this very capacity," observe; not "very will," or "very action;" for if he had said so much as this, he would clearly not be at variance with the teaching of the apostle. But there are his words: "this very capacity;" meaning that very one of the three faculties which he had placed in our nature. This God "evermore assists by the help of His grace." The result, indeed, is, that "the praise does not belong to man and to God," because man so wills that yet God also inspires his volition with the ardor of love, or that man so works that God nevertheless also cooperates with him, —and without His help, what is man? But he has associated God in this praise in this wise, that were it not for the nature which God gave us in our creation wherewith we might be able to exercise volition and action, we should neither will nor act.

Chapter 8. —Grace, According to the Pelagians, Consists in the Internal and Manifold Illumination of the Mind.

As to this natural capacity which, he allows, is assisted by the grace of God, it is by no means clear from the passage either what grace he means, or to what extent he supposes our nature to be assisted by it. But, as is the case in other passages in which he expresses himself with more clearness and decision, we may here also perceive that no other grace is intended by him as helping natural capacity than the law and the teaching. [VII.] For in one passage he says: "We are supposed by very ignorant persons to do wrong in this matter to divine grace, because we say that it by no means perfects sanctity in us without our will, —as if God could have imposed any command on His grace, without also supplying the help of His grace to those on whom he imposed His commands, so that men might more easily accomplish through grace what they are required to do by their free will." Then, as if he meant to explain what grace he meant, he immediately went on to add these words: "And this grace we for our part do not, as you suppose, allow to consist merely in the law, but also in the help of God." Now who can help wishing that he would show us what grace it is that he would have us understand? Indeed, we have the strongest reason for desiring him to tell us what he means by saying that he does not allow grace merely to consist in the law. Whilst, however, we are in the suspense of our expectation, observe, I pray you, what he has further to tell us: "God helps us," says he, "by His teaching and revelation, whilst He opens the eyes of our heart; whilst He points out to us the future, that we may not be absorbed in the present; whilst He discovers to us the snares of the devil; whilst He enlightens us with the manifold and ineffable gift of heavenly grace." He then concludes his statement with a kind of absolution: "Does the man," he asks, "who says all this appear to you to be a denier of grace? Does he not acknowledge both man's free will and God's grace?" But, after all, he has not got beyond his commendation of the law and of teaching; assiduously inculcating this as the grace that helps us, and so following up the idea with which he had started, when he said, "We, however, allow it to consist in the help of God." God's help, indeed, he supposed must be recommended to us by manifold lures; by setting forth teaching and revelation, the opening of the eyes of the heart, the demonstration of the future, the discovery of the devil's wiles, and the illumination of our minds by the varied and indescribable gift of heavenly grace, —all this, of course, with a view to our learning the commandments and promises of God. And what else is this than placing God's grace in "the law and the teaching"?

Chapter 9 [VIII.]—The Law One Thing, Grace Another. The Utility of the Law.

Hence, then, it is clear that he acknowledges that grace whereby God points out and reveals to us what we are bound to do; but not that whereby He endows and assists us to act, since the knowledge of the law, unless it be accompanied by the assistance of grace, rather avails for producing the transgression of the commandment. "Where there is no law," says the apostle, "there is no transgression;" and again: "I had not known lust except the law had said, Thou shalt not covet." Therefore, so far are the law and grace from being the same thing, that the law is not only unprofitable, but it is absolutely prejudicial, unless grace assists it; and the utility of the law may be shown by this, that it obliges all whom it proves guilty of transgression to betake themselves to grace for deliverance and help to overcome their evil lusts. For it rather commands than assists; it discovers disease, but does not heal it; nay, the malady that is not healed is rather aggravated by it, so that the cure of grace is more earnestly and anxiously sought for, inasmuch as "The letter kills, but the spirit gives life." "For if there had been a law given which could have given life, verily righteousness should have been by the law." To what extent, however, the law gives assistance, the apostle informs us when he says immediately afterwards: "The Scripture hath concluded all under sin, that the promise by faith of Jesus Christ might be given to them that believe." Wherefore, says the apostle, "the law was our schoolmaster in Christ Jesus." Now this very thing is serviceable to proud men, to be more firmly and manifestly "concluded under sin," so that none may presumptuously endeavor to accomplish their justification by means of free will as if by their own resources; but rather "that every mouth may be stopped, and all the world may become guilty before God. Because by the deeds of the law there shall no flesh be justified in His sight: for by the law is the knowledge of sin. But now the righteousness of God without the law is manifested, being witnessed by the law and the prophets." How then manifested without the law, if witnessed by the law? For this very reason the phrase is not, "manifested without the law," but "the righteousness without the law," because it is "the righteousness of God;" that is, the righteousness which we have not from the law, but from God,—not the righteousness, indeed, which by reason of His commanding it, causes us fear through our knowledge of it; but rather the righteous ness which by reason of His bestowing it, is held fast and maintained by us through our loving it,—"so that he that glories, let him glory in the Lord."

Chapter 10 [IX.]—What Purpose the Law Subserves.

What object, then, can this man gain by accounting the law and the teaching to be the grace whereby we are helped to work righteousness? For, in order that it may help much, it must help us to feel our need of grace. No man, indeed, can fulfil the law through the law. "Love is the fulfilling of the law." And the love of God is not shed abroad in our hearts by the law, but by the Holy Ghost, which is given unto us. Grace, therefore, is pointed at by the law, in order that the law may be fulfilled by grace. Now what does it avail for Pelagius, that he declares the self-same thing under different phrases, that he may not be understood to place in law and teaching that grace which, as he avers, assists the "capacity" of our nature? So far, indeed, as I can conjecture, the reason why he fears being so understood is, because he condemned all those who maintain that God's grace and help are not given for a man's single actions, but exist rather in his freedom, or in the law and teaching. And yet he supposes that he escapes detection by the shifts he so constantly employs for disguising what he means by his formula of "law and teaching" under so many various phrases.

Chapter 11 [X.]—Pelagius' Definition of How God Helps Us: "He Promises Us Future Glory."

For in another passage, after asserting at length that it is not by the help of God, but out of our own selves, that a good will is formed within us, he confronted himself with a question out of the apostle's epistle; and he asked this question: "How will this stand consistently with the apostle's words, 'It is God that worketh in you both to will and to perfect'?" Then, in order to obviate this opposing authority, which he plainly saw to be most thoroughly contrasted with his own dogma, he went on at once to add: "He works in us to will what is good, to will what is holy, when He rouses us from our devotion to earthly desires, and from our love of the present only, after the manner of brute animals, by the magnitude of the future glory and the promise of its rewards; when by revealing wisdom to us He stirs up our sluggish will to a longing after God; when (what you are not afraid to deny in another passage) he persuades us to everything which is good." Now what can be plainer, than that by the grace whereby God works within us to will what is good, he means nothing else than the law and the teaching? For in the law and the teaching of the holy Scriptures are promised future glory and its great rewards. To the teaching also appertains the revelation of wisdom, whilst it is its further function to direct our thoughts to everything that is good. And if between teaching and persuading (or rather exhorting) there seems to be a difference, yet even this is provided for in the general term "teaching," which is contained in the several discourses or letters; for the holy Scriptures both teach and exhort, and in the processes of teaching and exhorting there is room likewise for man's operation. We, however, on our side would fain have him sometime confess that grace, by which not only future glory in all its magnitude is promised, but also is believed in and hoped for; by which wisdom is not only revealed, but also loved; by which everything that is good is not only recommended, but pressed upon us until we accept it. For all men do not possess faith, who hear the Lord in the Scriptures promising the kingdom of heaven; nor are all men persuaded, who are counselled to come to Him, who says, "Come unto me, all ye that labor." They, however, who have faith are the same who are also persuaded to come to Him. This He Himself set forth most plainly, when He said, "No man can come to me, except the Father, which hath sent me, draw him." And some verses afterwards, when speaking of such as believe not, He says, "Therefore said I unto you, that no man can come unto me except it were given unto him of my Father." This is the grace which Pelagius ought to acknowledge, if he wishes not only to be called a Christian, but to be one.

Chapter 12 [XI.]—The Same Continued: "He Reveals Wisdom."

But what shall I say about the revelation of wisdom? For there is no man who can in the present life very well hope to attain to the great revelations which were given to the Apostle Paul; and of course it is impossible to suppose that anything was accustomed in these revelations to be made known to him but what appertained to wisdom. Yet for all this he says: "Lest I should be exalted above measure through the abundance of the revelations, there was given to me a thorn in the flesh, the messenger of Satan to buffet me. For this thing I besought the Lord thrice, that He would take it away from me. And He said unto me, My grace is sufficient for thee; for my strength is made perfect in weakness." Now, undoubtedly, if there were already in the apostle that perfection of love which admitted of no further addition, and which could be puffed up no more, there could have been no further need of the messenger of Satan to buffet him, and thereby to repress the excessive elation which might arise from abundance of revelations. What means this elation, however, but a being puffed up? And of love it has been indeed most truly said, "Love vaunted not itself, is not puffed up." This love, therefore, was still in process of constant increase in the great apostle, day by day, as long as his "inward man was renewed day by day," and would then be perfected, no doubt, when he was got beyond the reach of all further vaunting and elation. But at that time his mind was still in a condition to be inflated by an abundance of revelations before it was perfected in the solid edifice of love; for he had not arrived at the goal and apprehended the prize, to which he was reaching forward in his course.

Chapter 13 [XII.]—Grace Causes Us to Do.

To him, therefore, who is reluctant to endure the troublesome process, whereby this vaunting disposition is restrained, before he attains to the ultimate and highest perfection of charity, it is most properly said, "My grace is sufficient for thee; for my strength is made perfect in weakness,"—in weakness, that is, not of the flesh only, as this man supposes, but both of the flesh and of the mind; because the mind, too, was, in comparison of that last stage of complete perfection, weak, and to it also was assigned, in order to check its elation, that messenger of Satan, the thorn in the flesh; although it was very strong, in contrast with the carnal or animal faculties, which as yet understand not the things of the Spirit of God. Inasmuch, then, as strength is made perfect in weakness, whoever does not own himself to be weak, is not in the way to be perfected. This grace, however, by which strength is perfected in weakness, conducts all who are predestinated and called according to the divine purpose to the state of the highest perfection and glory. By such grace it is affected, not only that we discover what ought to be done, but also that we do what we have discovered, —not only that we believe what ought to be loved, but also that we love what we have believed.

Chapter 14 [XII.]—The Righteousness Which is of God, and the Righteousness Which is of the Law.

If this grace is to be called "teaching," let it at any rate be so called in such wise that God may be believed to infuse it, along with an ineffable sweetness, more deeply and more internally, not only by their agency who plant and water from without, but likewise by His own too who ministers in secret His own increase, —in such a way, that He not only exhibits truth, but likewise imparts love. For it is thus that God teaches those who have been called according to His purpose, giving them simultaneously both to know what they ought to do, and to do what they know. Accordingly, the apostle thus speaks to the Thessalonians: "As touching love of the brethren, ye need not that I write unto you; for ye yourselves are taught of God to love one another." And then, by way of proving that they had been taught of God, he subjoined: "And indeed ye do it towards all the brethren which are in all Macedonia." As if the surest sign that you have been taught of God, is that you put into practice what you have been taught. Of that character are all who are called according to God's purpose, as it is written in the prophets: "They shall be all taught of God." The man, however, who has learned what ought to be done, but does it not, has not as yet been "taught of God" according to grace, but only according to the law, —not according to the spirit, but only according to the letter. Although there are many who appear to do what the law commands, through fear of punishment, not through love of righteousness; and such righteousness as this the apostle calls "his own which is after the law,"—a thing as it were commanded, not given. When, indeed, it has been given, it is not called our own righteousness, but God's; because it becomes our own only so that we have it from God. These are the apostle's words: "That I may be found in Him, not having mine own righteousness which is of the law, but that which is through the faith of Christ the righteousness which is of God by faith." So great, then, is the difference between the law and grace, that although the law is undoubtedly of God, yet the righteousness which is "of the law" is not "of God," but the righteousness which is consummated by grace is "of God." The one is designated "the righteousness of the law," because it is done through fear of the curse of the law; while the other is called "the righteousness of God," because it is bestowed through the beneficence of His grace, so that it is not a terrible but a pleasant commandment, according to the prayer in the psalm: "Good art Thou, O Lord, therefore in Thy goodness teach me Thy righteousness;" that is, that I may not be compelled like a slave to live under the law with fear of punishment; but rather in the freedom of love may be delighted to live with law as my companion. When the freeman keeps a commandment, he does it readily. And whosoever learns his duty in this spirit, does everything that he has learned ought to be done.

Chapter 15 [XIV.]—He Who Has Been Taught by Grace Actually Comes to Christ.

Now as touching this kind of teaching, the Lord also says: "Every man that hath heard, and hath learned of the Father, cometh unto me." Of the man, therefore, who has not come, it cannot be correctly said: "Has heard and has learned that it is his duty to come to Him, but he is not willing to do what he has learned." It is indeed absolutely improper to apply such a statement to that method of teaching, whereby God teaches by grace. For if, as the Truth says, "Every man that hath learned cometh," it follows, of course, that whoever does not come has not learned. But who can fail to see that a man's coming or not coming is by the determination of his will? This determination, however, may stand alone, if the man does not come; but if he does come, it cannot be without assistance; and such assistance, that he not only knows what it is he ought to do, but also actually does what he thus knows. And thus, when God teaches, it is not by the letter of the law, but by the grace of the Spirit. Moreover, He so teaches, that whatever a man learns, he not only sees with his perception, but also desires with his choice, and accomplishes in action. By this mode, therefore, of divine instruction, volition itself, and performance itself, are assisted, and not merely the natural "capacity" of willing and performing. For if nothing but this "capacity" of ours were assisted by this grace, the Lord would rather have said, "Every man that hath heard and hath learned of the Father may possibly come unto me." This, however, is not what He said; but His words are these: "Every man that hath heard and hath learned of the Father come unto me." Now the possibility of coming Pelagius places in nature, or even—as we found him attempting to say some time ago—in grace (whatever that may mean according to him), —when he says, "whereby this very capacity is assisted;" whereas the actual coming lies in the will and act. It does not, however, follow that he who may come actually comes, unless he has also willed and acted for the coming. But everyone who has learned of the Father not only has the possibility of coming, but comes; and in this result are already included the motion of the capacity, the affection of the will, and the effect of the action.

Chapter 16 [XV.]—We Need Divine Aid in the Use of Our Powers. Illustration from Sight.

Now what is the use of his examples, if they do not really accomplish his own promise of making his meaning clearer to us; not, indeed, that we are bound to admit their sense, but that we may discover more plainly and openly what is his drift and purpose in using them? "That we are able," says he, "to see with our eyes is not of us; but it is of us that we make a good or a bad use of our sight." Well, there is an answer for him in the psalm, in which the psalmist says to God, "Turn Thou away mine eyes, that they behold not iniquity." Now although this was said of the eyes of the mind, it still follows from it, that in respect of our bodily eyes there is either a good use or a bad use that may be made of them: not in the literal sense merely of a good sight when the eyes are sound, and a bad sight when they are bleared, but in the moral sense of a right sight when it is directed towards succoring the helpless, or a bad sight when its object is the indulgence of lust. For although both the pauper who is succored, and the woman who is lusted after, are seen by these external eyes; it is after all from the inner eyes that either compassion in the one case or lust in the other proceeds. How then is it that the prayer is offered to God, "Turn Thou away mine eyes, that they behold not iniquity"? Or why is that asked for which lies within our own power, if it be true that God does not assist the will?

Chapter 17 [XVI.]—Does Pelagius Designedly Refrain from Openly Saying that All Good Action is from God?

"That we are able to speak," says he, "is of God; but that we make a good or a bad use of speech is of ourselves." He, however, who has made the most excellent use of speech does not teach us so. "For," says He, "it is not ye that speak, but the Spirit of your Father that speaks in you." "So, again," adds Pelagius, "that I may, by applying a general case in illustration, embrace all, —that we are able to do, say, think, any good thing, comes from Him who has endowed us with this ability, and who also assists it." Observe how even here he repeats his former meaning —that of these three, capacity, volition, action, it is only the capacity which receives help. Then, by way of completely stating what he intends to say, he adds: "But that we really do a good thing, or speak a good word, or think a good thought, proceeds from our own selves." He forgot what he had before said by way of correcting, as it were, his own words; for after saying, "Man is to be praised therefore for his willing and doing a good work," he at once goes on to modify his statement thus: "Or rather, this praise belongs both to man, and to God who has given him the capacity of this very will and work." Now what is the reason why he did not remember this admission when giving his examples, so as to say this much at least after quoting them: "That we are able to do, say, think any good thing, comes from Him who has given us this ability, and who also assists it. That, however, we really do a good thing, or speak a good word, or think a good thought, proceeds both from ourselves and from Him!" This, however, he has not said.

But, if I am not mistaken, I think I see why he was afraid to do so.

Chapter 18 [XVII.]—He Discovers the Reason of Pelagius' Hesitation So to Say.

For, when wishing to point out why this lies within our own competency, he says: "Because we are able to turn all these actions into evil." This, then, was the reason why he was afraid to admit that such an action proceeds "both from ourselves and from God," lest it should be objected to him in reply: "If the fact of our doing, speaking, thinking anything good, is owing both to ourselves and to God, because He has endowed us with this ability, then it follows that our doing, thinking, speaking evil things, is due to ourselves and to God, because He has here also endowed us with ability of indifferency; the conclusion from this being—and God forbid that we should admit any such—that just as God is associated with ourselves in the praise of good actions, so must He share with us the blame of evil actions." For that "capacity" with which He has endowed us makes us capable alike of good actions and of evil ones.

Chapter 19 [XVIII.]—The Two Roots of Action, Love and Cupidity; And Each Brings Forth Its Own Fruit.

Concerning this "capacity," Pelagius thus writes in the first book of his Defense of Free Will: "Now," says he, "we have implanted in us by God a capacity for either part. It resembles, as I may say, a fruitful and fecund root which yields and produces diversely according to the will of man, and which is capable, at the planter's own choice, of either shedding a beautiful bloom of virtues, or of bristling with the thorny thickets of vices." Scarcely heeding what he says, he here makes one and the same root productive both of good and evil fruits, in opposition to gospel truth and apostolic teaching. For the Lord declares that "a good tree cannot bring forth evil fruit, neither can a corrupt tree bring forth good fruit;" and when the Apostle Paul says that covetousness is "the root of all evils," he intimates to us, of course, that love may be regarded as the root of all good things. On the supposition, therefore, that two trees, one good and the other corrupt, represent two human beings, a good one and a bad, what else is the good man except one with a good will, that is, a tree with a good root? And what is the bad man except one with a bad will, that is, a tree with a bad root? The fruits which spring from such roots and trees are deeds, are words, are thoughts, which proceed, when good, from a good will, and when evil, from an evil one.

Chapter 20 [XIX.]—How a Man Makes a Good or a Bad Tree.

Now a man makes a good tree when he receives the grace of God. For it is not by himself that he makes himself good instead of evil; but it is of Him, and through Him, and in Him who is always good. And in order that he may not only be a good tree, but also bear good fruit, it is necessary for him to be assisted by the self-same grace, without which he can do nothing good. For God Himself cooperates in the production of fruit in good trees, when He both externally waters and tends them by the agency of His servants, and internally by Himself also gives the increase. A man, however, makes a corrupt tree when he makes himself corrupt, when he falls away from Him who is the unchanging good; for such a declension from Him is the origin of an evil will. Now this decline does not initiate some other corrupt nature, but it corrupts that which has been already created good. When this corruption, however, has been healed, no evil remains; for although nature no doubt had received an injury, yet nature was not itself a blemish.

Chapter 21 [XX.]—Love the Root of All Good Things; Cupidity, of All Evil Ones.

The "capacity," then, of which we speak is not (as he supposes) the one identical root both of good things and evil. For the love which is the root of good things is quite different from the cupidity which is the root of evil things—as different, indeed, as virtue is from vice. But without doubt this "capacity" is capable of either root: because a man is not only able to possess love, whereby the tree becomes a good one; but he is likewise able to have cupidity, which makes the tree evil. This human cupidity, however, which is a vice, has for its author man, or man's deceiver, but not man's Creator. It is indeed that "lust of the flesh, and the lust of the eyes, and the pride of life, which is not of the Father, but is of the world." And who can be ignorant of the usage of the Scripture, which under the designation of "the world" is accustomed to describe those who inhabit the world?

Chapter 22 [XXI.]—Love is a Good Will.

That love, however, which is a virtue, comes to us from God, not from ourselves, according to the testimony of Scripture, which says: "Love is of God; and every one that loves is born of God, and knows God: for God is love." It is on the principle of this love that one can best understand the passage, "Whosoever is born of God doth not commit sin;" as well as the sentence, "And he cannot sin." Because the love according to which we are born of God "doth not behave itself unseemly," and "thinketh no evil." Therefore, whenever a man sins, it is not according to love: but it is according to cupidity that he commits sin; and following such a disposition, he is not born of God. Because, as it has been already stated, "the capacity" of which we speak is capable of either root. When, therefore, the Scripture says, "Love is of God," or still more pointedly, "God is love;" when the Apostle John so very emphatically exclaims, "Behold what manner of love the Father hath bestowed upon us, that we should be called, and be, the sons of God!" with what face can this writer, on hearing that "God is love," persist in maintaining his opinion, that we bare of God one only of those three, namely, "the capacity;" whereas it is of ourselves that we have "the good will" and "the good action?" As if, indeed, this good will were a different thing from that love which the Scripture so loudly proclaims to have come to us from God, and to have been given to us by the Father, that we might become His children.

Chapter 23 [XXII.]—Pelagius' Double Dealing Concerning the Ground of the Conferrence of Grace.

Perhaps, however, our own antecedent merits caused this gift to be bestowed upon us; as this writer has already suggested about God's grace, in that work which he addressed to a holy virgin, whom he mentions in the letter sent by him to Rome. For, after adducing the testimony of the Apostle James, in which he says, "Submit yourselves unto God; but resist the devil, and he will flee from you," he goes on to say: "He shows us how we ought to resist the devil, if we submit ourselves indeed to God and by doing His will merit His divine grace, and by the help of the Holy Ghost more easily withstand the evil spirit." Judge, then, how sincere was his condemnation in the Palestine Synod of those persons who say that God's grace is conferred on us according to our merits! Have we any doubt as to his still holding this opinion, and most openly proclaiming it? Well, how could that confession of his before the bishops have been true and real? Had he already written the book in which he most explicitly alleges that grace is bestowed on us according to our deserts—the very position which he without any reservation condemned at that Synod in the East? Let him frankly acknowledge that he once held the opinion, but that he holds it no longer; so should we most frankly rejoice in his improvement. As it is, however, when, besides other objections, this one was laid to his charge which we are now discussing, he said in reply: "Whether these are the opinions of Cœlestius or not, is the concern of those who affirm that they are. For my own part, indeed, I never entertained such views; on the contrary, I anathematize everyone who does entertain them." But how could he "never have entertained such views," when he had already composed this work? Or how does he still "anathematize everybody who entertains these views," if he afterwards composed this work?

Chapter 24. —Pelagius Places Free Will at the Basis of All Turning to God for Grace.

But perhaps he may meet us with this rejoinder, that in the sentence before us he spoke of our "meriting the divine grace by doing the will of God," in the sense that grace is added to those who believe and lead godly lives, whereby they may boldly withstand the tempter; whereas their very first reception of grace was, that they might do the will of God. Lest, then, he makes such a rejoinder, consider some other words of his on this subject: "The man," says he, "who hastens to the Lord, and desires to be directed by Him, that is, who makes his own will depend upon God's, who moreover cleaves so closely to the Lord as to become (as the apostle says) 'one spirit' with Him, does all this by nothing else than by his freedom of will." Observe how great a result he has here stated to be accomplished only by our freedom of will; and how, in fact, he supposes us to cleave to God without the help of God: for such is the force of his words, "by nothing else than by his own freedom of will." So that, after we have cleaved to the Lord without His help, we even then, because of such adhesion of our own, deserve to be assisted. [XXIII.] For he goes on to say: "Whosoever makes a right use of this" (that is, rightly uses his freedom of will), "does so entirely surrender himself to God, and does so completely mortify his own will, that he is able to say with the apostle, 'Nevertheless it is already not I that live, but Christ lives in me;' and 'He placed his heart in the hand of God, so that He turned it whithersoever He wills.'" Great indeed is the help of the grace of God, so that He turns our heart in whatever direction He pleases. But according to this writer's foolish opinion, however great the help may be, we deserve it all at the moment when, without any assistance beyond the liberty of our will, we hasten to the Lord, desire His guidance and direction, suspend our own will entirely on His, and by close adherence to Him become one spirit with Him. Now all these vast courses of goodness we (according to him) accomplish, forsooth, simply by the freedom of our own free will; and because of such antecedent merits we so secure His grace, that He turns our heart which way so ever He pleases. Well, now, how is that grace which is not gratuitously conferred? How can it be grace, if it is given in payment of a debt? How can that be true which the apostle says, "It is not of yourselves, but it is the gift of God; not of works, lest any man should boast;" and again, "If it is of grace, then is it no more of works, otherwise grace is no more grace:" how, I repeat, can this be true, if such meritorious works precede as to procure for us the bestowal of grace? Surely, under the circumstances, there can be no gratuitous gift, but only the recompense of a due reward. Is it the case, then, that in order to find their way to the help of God, men run to God without God's help? And in order that we may receive God's help while cleaving to Him, do we without His help cleave to God? What greater gift, or even what similar gift, could grace itself bestow upon any man, if he has already without grace been able to make himself one spirit with the Lord by no other power than that of his own free will?

Chapter 25 [XXIV.]—God by His Wonderful Power Works in Our Hearts Good Dispositions of Our Will.

Now I want him to tell us whether that king of Assyria, whose holy wife Esther "abhorred his bed," whilst sitting upon the throne of his kingdom, and clothed in all his glorious apparel, adorned all over with gold and precious stones, and dreadful in his majesty when he raised his face, which was inflamed with anger, in the midst of his splendor, and beheld her, with the glare of a wild bull in the fierceness of his indignation; and the queen was afraid, and her color changed as she fainted, and she bowed herself upon the head of the maid that went before her; —I want him to tell us whether this king had yet "hastened to the Lord, and had desired to be directed by Him, and had subordinated his own will to His, and had, by cleaving fast to God, become one spirit with Him, simply by the force of his own free will." Had he surrendered himself wholly to God, and entirely mortified his own will, and placed his heart in the hand of God? I suppose that anybody who should think this of the king, in the state he was then in, would be not foolish only, but even mad. And yet God converted him, and turned his indignation into gentleness. Who, however, can fail to see how much greater a task it is to change and turn wrath completely into gentleness, than to bend the heart to something, when it is not preoccupied with either affection, but is indifferently poised between the two? Let them therefore read and understand, observe and acknowledge, that it is not by law and teaching uttering their lessons from without, but by a secret, wonderful, and ineffable power operating within, that God works in men's hearts not only revelations of the truth, but also good dispositions of the will.

Chapter 26 [XXV.]—The Pelagian Grace of "Capacity" Exploded. The Scripture Teaches the Need of God's Help in Doing, Speaking, and Thinking, Alike.

Let Pelagius, therefore, cease at last to deceive both himself and others by his disputations against the grace of God. It is not because only one of these three—that is to say, of the "capacity" of a good will and work—that the grace of God towards us ought to be proclaimed; but also because the good "will" and "work" themselves. This "capacity," indeed, according to his definition, avails for both directions; and yet our sins must not also be attributed to God in consequence, as our good actions, according to his view, are attributed to Him owing to the same capacity. It is not only, therefore, on this account that the help of God's grace is maintained, because it assists our natural capacity. He must cease to say, "That we are able to do, say, think any good, is from Him who has given us this ability, and who also assists this ability; whereas that we really do a good thing, or speak a good word, or think a good thought, proceeds from our own selves." He must, I repeat, cease to say this. For God has not only given us the ability and aids it, but He further works in us "to will and to do." It is not because we do not will, or do not do, that we will and do nothing good, but because we are without His help. How can he say, "That we are able to do good is of God, but that we actually do it is of ourselves," when the apostle tells us that he "prays to God" in behalf of those to whom he was writing, "that they should do no evil, but that they should do that which is good?" His words are not, "We pray that ye be able to do nothing evil;" but, "that ye do no evil." Neither does he say, "that ye be able to do good;" but, "that ye do good." Forasmuch as it is written, "As many as are led by the Spirit of God, they are the sons of God," it follows that, in order that they may do that which is good, they must be led by Him who is good. How can Pelagius say, "That we are able to make a good use of speech comes from God; but that we do actually make this good use of speech proceeds from ourselves," when the Lord declares, "It is the Spirit of your Father which speaks in you"? He does not say, "It is not you who have given to yourselves the power of speaking well;" but His words are, "It is not ye that speak." Nor does He say, "It is the Spirit of your Father which giveth, or hath given, you the power to speak well;" but He says, "which speaks in you." He does not allude to the motion of "the capacity," but He asserts the effect of the co-operation. How can this arrogant asserter of free will say, "That we are able to think a good thought comes from God, but that we actually think a good thought proceeds from ourselves"? He has his answer from the humble preacher of grace, who says, "Not that we are sufficient of ourselves to think anything as of ourselves, but our sufficiency is of God." Observe he does not say, "to be able to think anything;" but, "to think anything."

Chapter 27 [XXVI.]—What True Grace Is, and Wherefore Given. Merits Do Not Precede Grace.

Now even Pelagius should frankly confess that this grace is plainly set forth in the inspired Scriptures; nor should he with shameless effrontery hide the fact that he has too long opposed it, but admit it with salutary regret; so that the holy Church may cease to be harassed by his stubborn persistence, and rather rejoice in his sincere conversion. Let him distinguish between knowledge and love, as they ought to be distinguished; because "knowledge puffed up, but love edifies." And then knowledge no longer puffed up when love builds up. And inasmuch as each is the gift of God (although one is less, and the other greater), he must not extol our righteousness above the praise which is due to Him who justifies us, in such a way as to assign to the lesser of these two gifts the help of divine grace, and to claim the greater one for the human will. And should he consent that we receive love from the grace of God, he must not suppose that any merits of our own preceded our reception of the gift. For what merits could we possibly have had at the time when we loved not God? In order, indeed, that we might receive that love whereby we might love, we were loved while as yet we had no love ourselves. This the Apostle John most expressly declares: "Not that we loved God," says he, "but that He loved us;" and again, "We love Him, because He first loved us." Most excellently and truly spoken! For we could not have wherewithal to love Him, unless we received it from Him in His first loving us. And what good could we possibly do if we possessed no love? Or how could we help doing good if we have love? For although God's commandment appears sometimes to be kept by those who do not love Him, but only fear Him; yet where there is no love, no good work is imputed, nor is there any good work, rightly so called; because "whatsoever is not of faith is sin," and "faith worketh by love." Hence also that grace of God, whereby "His love is shed abroad in our hearts through the Holy Ghost, which is given unto us," must be so confessed by the man who would make a true confession, as to show his undoubting belief that nothing whatever in the way of goodness pertaining to godliness and real holiness can be accomplished without it. Not after the fashion of him who clearly enough shows us what he thinks of it when he says, that "grace is bestowed in order that what God commands may be the more easily fulfilled;" which of course means, that even without grace God's commandments may, although less easily, yet actually, be accomplished.

Chapter 28 [XXVII.]—Pelagius Teaches that Satan May Be Resisted Without the Help of the Grace of God.

In the book which he addressed to a certain holy virgin, there is a passage which I have already mentioned, wherein he plainly indicates what he holds on this subject; for he speaks of our "deserving the grace of God, and by the help of the Holy Ghost more easily resisting the evil spirit." Now why did he insert the phrase "more easily"? Was not the sense already complete: "And by the help of the Holy Ghost resisting the evil spirit"? But who can fail to perceive what an injury he has done by this insertion? He wants it, of course, to be supposed, that so great are the powers of our nature, which he is in such a hurry to exalt, that even without the assistance of the Holy Ghost the evil spirit can be resisted—less easily it may be, but still in a certain measure.

Chapter 29 [XXVIII.]—When He Speaks of God's Help, He Means It Only to Help Us Do What Without It We Still Could Do.

Again, in the first book of his Defense of the Freedom of the Will, he says: "But while we have within us a free will so strong and so steadfast against sinning, which our Maker has implanted in human nature generally, still, by His unspeakable goodness, we are further defended by His own daily help." What need is there of such help, if free will is so strong and so steadfast against sinning? But here, as before, he would have it understood that the purpose of the alleged assistance is, that that may be more easily accomplished by grace which he nevertheless supposes may be affected, less easily, no doubt, but yet actually, without grace.

Chapter 30 [XXIX.]—What Pelagius Thinks is Needful for Ease of Performance is Really Necessary for the Performance.

In like manner, in another passage of the same book, he says: "In order that men may more easily accomplish by grace that which they are commanded to do by free will." Now, expunge the phrase "more easily," and you leave not only a full, but also a sound sense, if it be regarded as meaning simply this: "That men may accomplish through grace what they are commanded to do by free will." The addition of the words "more easily," however, tacitly suggests the possibility of accomplishing good works even without the grace of God. But such a meaning is disallowed by Him who says, "Without me ye can do nothing."

Chapter 31 [XXX.]—Pelagius and Cœlestius Nowhere Really Acknowledge Grace.

Let him amend all this, that if human infirmity has erred in subjects so profound, he may not add to the error diabolical deception and willfulness, either by denying what he has really believed, or by maintaining what he has rashly believed, after he has once discovered, on recollecting the light of truth, that he ought never to have so believed. As for that grace, indeed, by which we are justified, —in other words, whereby "the love of God is shed abroad in our hearts by the Holy Ghost, which is given unto us,"—I have nowhere, in those writings of Pelagius and Cœlestius which I have had the opportunity of reading, found them acknowledging it as it ought to be acknowledged. In no passage at all have I observed them recognizing "the children of the promise," concerning whom the apostle thus speaks: "They which are children of the flesh, these are not the children of God; but the children of the promise are counted for the seed." For that which God promises we do not ourselves bring about by our own choice or natural power, but He Himself effects it by grace.

Chapter 32. —Why the Pelagians Deemed Prayers to Be Necessary. The Letter Which Pelagius Dispatched to Pope Innocent with an Exposition of His Belief.

Now I will say nothing at present about the works of Cœlestius, or those tracts of his which he produced in those ecclesiastical proceedings, copies of the whole of which we have taken care to send to you, along with another letter which we deemed it necessary to add. If you carefully examine all these documents, you will observe that he does not posit the grace of God, which helps us whether to avoid evil or to do good, beyond the natural choice of the will, but only in the law and teaching. Thus he even asserts that their very prayers are necessary for the purpose of showing men what to desire and love. All these documents, however, I may omit further notice of at present; for Pelagius himself has lately forwarded to Rome both a letter and an exposition of his belief, addressing it to Pope Innocent, of blessed memory, of whose death he was ignorant. Now in this letter he says that "there are certain subjects about which some men are trying to vilify him. One of these is, that he refuses to infants the sacrament of baptism, and promises the kingdom of heaven to some, independently of Christ's redemption. Another of them is, that he so speaks of man's ability to avoid sin as to exclude God's help, and so strongly confides in free will that he repudiates the help of divine grace." Now, as touching the perverted opinion he holds about the baptism of infants (although he allows that it ought to be administered to them), in opposition to the Christian faith and catholic truth, this is not the place for us to enter on an accurate discussion, for we must now complete our treatise on the assistance of grace, which is the subject we undertook. Let us see what answer he makes out of this very letter to the objection which he has proposed concerning this matter. Omitting his invidious complaints about his opponents, we approach the subject before us; and find him expressing himself as follows.

Chapter 33 [XXXI.]—Pelagius Professes Nothing on the Subject of Grace Which May Not Be Understood of the Law and Teaching.

"See," he says, "how this epistle will clear me before your Blessedness; for in it we clearly and simply declare, that we possess a free will which is unimpaired for sinning and for not sinning; and this free will is in all good works always assisted by divine help." Now you perceive, by the understanding which the Lord has given you, that these words of his are inadequate to solve the question. For it is still open to us to inquire what the help is by which he would say that the free will is assisted; lest perchance he should, as is usual with him, maintain that law and teaching are meant. If, indeed, you were to ask him why he used the word "always," he might answer: Because it is written, And in His law will he meditate day and night." Then, after interposing a statement about the condition of man, and his natural capacity for sinning and not sinning, he added the following words: "Now this power of free will we declare to reside generally in all alike—in Christians, in Jews, and in Gentiles. In all men free will exists equally by nature, but in Christians alone is it assisted by grace." We again ask: "By what grace?" And again he might answer: "By the law and the Christian teaching."

Chapter 34.—Pelagius Says that Grace is Given According to Men's Merits. The Beginning, However, of Merit is Faith; And This is a Gratuitous Gift, Not a Recompense for Our Merits.

Then, again, whatever it is which he means by "grace," he says is given even to Christians according to their merits, although (as I have already mentioned above), when he was in Palestine, in his very remarkable vindication of himself, he condemned those who hold this opinion. Now these are his words: "In the one," says he, "the good of their created condition is naked and defenseless;" meaning in those who are not Christians. Then adding the rest: "In these, however, who belong to Christ, there is defense afforded by Christ's help." You see it is still uncertain what the help is, according to the remark we have already made on the same subject. He goes on, however, to say of those who are not Christians: "Those deserve judgment and condemnation, because, although they possess free will whereby they could come to have faith and deserve God's grace, they make a bad use of the freedom which has been granted to them. But these deserve to be rewarded, who by the right use of free will merit the Lord's grace, and keep His commandments." Now it is clear that he says grace is bestowed according to merit, whatever and of what kind so ever the grace is which he means, but which he does not plainly declare. For when he speaks of those persons as deserving reward who make a good use of their free will, and as therefore meriting the Lord's grace, he asserts in fact that a debt is paid to them. What, then, becomes of the apostle's saying, "Being justified freely by His grace"? And what of his other statement too, "By grace are ye saved"? —where, that he might prevent men's supposing that it is by works, he expressly added, "by faith." And yet further, lest it should be imagined that faith itself is to be attributed to men independently of the grace of God, the apostle says: "And that not of yourselves; for it is the gift of God." It follows, therefore, that we receive, without any merit of our own, that from which everything which, according to them, we obtain because of our merit, has its beginning—that is, faith itself. If, however, they insist on denying that this is freely given to us, what is the meaning of the apostle's words: "According as God hath dealt to every man the measure of faith"? But if it is contended that faith is so bestowed as to be a recompense for merit, not a free gift, what then becomes of another saying of the apostle: "Unto you it is given in the behalf of Christ, not only to believe in Him, but also to suffer for His sake"? Each is by the apostle's testimony made a gift, —both that he believes in Christ, and that each suffers for His sake. These men however, attribute faith to free will in such a way as to make it appear that grace is rendered to faith not as a gratuitous gift, but as a debt—thus ceasing to be grace any longer, because that is not grace which is not gratuitous.

Chapter 35 [XXXII.]—Pelagius Believes that Infants Have No Sin to Be Remitted in Baptism.

But Pelagius would have the reader pass from this letter to the book which states his belief. This he has made mention of to yourselves, and in it he has discoursed a good deal on points about which no question was raised as to his views. Let us, however, look simply at the subjects about which our own controversy with them is concerned. Having, then terminated a discussion which he had conducted to his heart's content, —from the Unity of the Trinity to the resurrection of the flesh, on which nobody was questioning him, —he goes on to say: "We hold likewise one baptism, which we aver ought to be administered to infants in the same sacramental formula as it is to adults." Well, now, you have yourselves affirmed that you heard him admit at least as much as this in your presence. What, however, is the use of his saying that the sacrament of baptism is administered to children "in the same words as it is to adults," when our inquiry concerns the thing, not merely the words? It is a more important matter, that (as you write) with his own mouth he replied to your own question, that "infants receive baptism for the remission of sins." For he did not say here, too, "in words of remission of sins," but he acknowledged that they are baptized for the remission itself; and yet for all this, if you were to ask him what the sin is which he supposes to be remitted to them, he would contend that they had none whatever.

Chapter 36 [XXXIII.]—Cœlestius Openly Declares Infants to Have No Original Sin.

Who would believe that, under so clear a confession, there is concealed a contrary meaning, if Cœlestius had not exposed it? He who in that book of his, which he quoted at Rome in the ecclesiastical proceedings there, distinctly acknowledged that "infants too are baptized for the remission of sins," also denied "that they have any original sin." But let us now observe what Pelagius thought, not about the baptism of infants, but rather about the assistance of divine grace, in this exposition of his belief which he forwarded to Rome. "We confess," says he, "free will in such a sense that we declare ourselves to be always in need of the help of God." Well, now, we ask again, what the help is which he says we require; and again we find ambiguity, since he may possibly answer that he meant the law and the teaching of Christ, whereby that natural "capacity" is assisted. We, however, on our side require them to acknowledge a grace like that which the apostle describes, when he says: "For God hath not given us the spirit of fear; but of power, and of love, and of a sound mind;" although it does not follow by any means that the man who has the gift of knowledge, whereby he has discovered what he ought to do, has also the grace of love so as to do it.

Chapter 37 [XXXIV.]—Pelagius Nowhere Admits the Need of Divine Help for Will and Action.

I also have read those books or writings of his which he mentions in the letter which he sent to Pope Innocent, of blessed memory, with the exception of a brief epistle which he says he sent to the holy Bishop Constantius; but I have nowhere been able to find in them that he acknowledges such a grace as helps not only that "natural capacity of willing and acting" (which according to him we possess, even when we neither will a good thing nor do it), but also the will and the action itself, by the ministration of the Holy Ghost.

Chapter 38 [XXXV.]—A Definition of the Grace of Christ by Pelagius.

"Let them read," says he, "the epistle which we wrote about twelve years ago to that holy man Bishop Paulinus: its subject throughout in some three hundred lines is the confession of God's grace and assistance alone, and our own inability to do any good thing at all without God." Well, I have read this epistle also, and found him dwelling throughout it on scarcely any other topic than the faculty and capacity of nature, whilst he makes God's grace consist almost entirely in this. Christ's grace, indeed, he treats with great brevity, simply mentioning its name, so that his only aim seems to have been to avoid the scandal of ignoring it altogether. It is, however, absolutely uncertain whether he means Christ's grace to consist in the remission of sins, or even in the teaching of Christ, including also the example of His life (a meaning which he asserts in several passages of his treatises); or whether he believes it to be a help towards good living, in addition to nature and teaching, through the inspiring influence of a burning and shining love.

Chapter 39 [XXXVI]—A Letter of Pelagius Unknown to Augustin.

"Let them also read," says he, "my epistle to the holy Bishop Constantius, wherein I have—briefly no doubt, but yet plainly—conjoined the grace and help of God with man's free will." This epistle, as I have already stated, I have not read; but if it is not unlike the other writings which he mentions, and with which I am acquainted, even this work does nothing for the subject of our present inquiry.

Chapter 40 [XXXVII]—The Help of Grace Placed by Pelagius in the Mere Revelation of Teaching.

"Let them read moreover" says he, "what I wrote, when I was in the East, to Christ's holy virgin Demetrias, and they will find that we so commend the nature of man as always to add the help of God's grace." Well, I read this letter too; and it had almost persuaded me that he did acknowledge therein the grace about which our discussion is concerned, although he did certainly seem in many passages of this work to contradict himself. But when there also came to my hands those other treatises which he afterwards wrote for more extensive circulation, I discovered in what sense he must have intended to speak of grace, —concealing what he believed under an ambiguous generality, but employing the term "grace" in order to break the force of obloquy, and to avoid giving offence. For at the very commencement of this work (where he says: "Let us apply ourselves with all earnestness to the task which we have set before us, nor let us have any misgiving because of our own humble ability; for we believe that we are assisted by the mother's faith and her daughter's merit") he appeared to me at first to acknowledge the grace which helps us to individual action; nor did I notice at once the fact that he might possibly have made this grace consist simply in the revelation of teaching.

Chapter 41. —Restoration of Nature Understood by Pelagius as Forgiveness of Sins.

In this same work he says in another passage: "Now, if even without God men show of what character they have been made by God, see what Christians have it in their power to do, whose nature has been through Christ restored to a better condition, and who are, moreover, assisted by the help of divine grace." By this restoration of nature to a better state he would have us understand the remission of sins. This he has shown with sufficient clearness in another passage of this epistle, where he says: "Even those who have become in a certain sense obdurate through their long practice of sinning, can be restored through repentance." But he may even here too make the assistance of divine grace consist in the revelation of teaching.

Chapter 42 [XXXVIII.]—Grace Placed by Pelagius in the Remission of Sins and the Example of Christ.

Likewise, in another place in this epistle of his he says: "Now, if even before the law, as we have already remarked, and long before the coming of our Lord and Savior, some men are related to have lived righteous and holy lives; how much worthier of belief is it that we can do this since the illumination of His coming, who have been restored by the grace of Christ, and born again into a better man? How much better than they, who lived before the law, ought we to be, who have been reconciled and cleansed by His blood, and by His example encouraged to the perfection of righteousness!" Observe how even here, although in different language, he has made the assistance of grace to consist in the remission of sins and the example of Christ. He then completes the passage by adding these words: "Better than they were even who lived under the law; according to the apostle, who says, 'Sin shall not have dominion over you: for ye are not under the law, but under grace.' Now, inasmuch as we have," says he, "said enough, as I suppose, on this point, let us describe a perfect virgin, who shall testify the good at once of nature and of grace by the holiness of her conduct, evermore warmed with the virtues of both." Now you ought to notice that in these words also he wished to conclude what he was saying in such a way that we might understand the good of nature to be that which we received when we were created; but the good of grace to be that which we receive when we regard and follow the example of Christ,—as if sin were not permitted to those who were or are under the law, on this account, because they either had not Christ's example, or else do not believe in Him.

Chapter 43 [XXXIX.]—The Forgiveness of Sins and Example of Christ Held by Pelagius Enough to Save the Most Hardened Sinner.

That this, indeed, is his meaning, other words also of his show us, —not contained in this work, but in the third book of his Defense of Free Will, wherein he holds a discussion with an opponent, who had insisted on the apostle's words when he says, "For what I would, that do I not;" and again, "I see another law in my members, warring against the law of my mind." To this he replied in these words: "Now that which you wish us to understand of the apostle himself, all Church writers assert that he spoke in the person of the sinner, and of one who was still under the law, —such a man as was, because of a very long custom of vice, held bound, as it were, by a certain necessity of sinning, and who, although he desired good with his will, in practice indeed was hurried headlong into evil. In the person, however, of one man," he continues, "the apostle designates the people who still sinned under the ancient law. This nation he declares was to be delivered from this evil of custom through Christ, who first of all remits all sins in baptism to those who believe in Him, and then urges them by an imitation of Himself to perfect holiness, and by the example of His own virtues overcomes the evil custom of their sins." Observe in what way he supposes them to be assisted who sin under the law: they are to be delivered by being justified through Christ's grace, as if the law alone were insufficient for them, without some reinforcement from Christ, owing to their long habit of sinning; not the inspiration of love by His Holy Spirit, but the contemplation and copy of His example in the inculcation of virtue by the gospel. Now here, at any rate, there was the very greatest call on him to say plainly what grace he meant, seeing that the apostle closed the very passage which formed the ground of discussion with these telling words: "O wretched man that I am, who shall deliver me from the body of this death? The grace of God, through Jesus Christ our Lord." Now, when he places this grace, not in the aid of His power, but in His example for imitation, what further hope must we entertain of him, since everywhere the word "grace" is mentioned by him under an ambiguous generality?

Chapter 44 [XL.]—Pelagius Once More Guards Himself Against the Necessity of Grace.

Then, again, in the work addressed to the holy virgin, of which we have spoken already, there is this passage: "Let us submit ourselves to God, and by doing His will let us merit the divine grace; and let us the more easily, by the help of the Holy Ghost, resist the evil spirit." Now, in these words of his, it is plain enough that he regards us as assisted by the grace of the Holy Ghost, not because we are unable to resist the tempter without Him by the sheer capacity of our nature, but in order that we may resist more easily. With respect, however, to the quantity and quality, whatever these might be, of this assistance, we may well believe that he made them consist of the additional knowledge which the Spirit reveals to us through teaching, and which we either cannot, or scarcely can, possess by nature. Such are the particulars which I have been able to discover in the book which he addressed to the virgin of Christ, and wherein he seems to confess grace. Of what purport and kind these are, you of course perceive.

Chapter 45 [XLI.]—To What Purpose Pelagius Thought Prayers Ought to Be Offered.

"Let them also read," says he, "my recent little treatise which we were obliged to publish a short while ago in defense of free will, and let them acknowledge how unfair is their determination to disparage us for a denial of grace, when we throughout almost the whole work acknowledge fully and sincerely both free will and grace." There are four books in this treatise, all of which I read, marking such passages as required consideration, and which I proposed to discuss: these I examined as well as I was able, before we came to that epistle of his which was sent to Rome. But even in these four books, that which he seems to regard as the grace which helps us to turn aside from evil and to do good, he describes in such a manner as to keep to his old ambiguity of language, and thus have it in his power so to explain to his followers, that they may suppose the assistance which is rendered by grace, for the purpose of helping our natural capacity, consists of nothing else than the law and the teaching. Thus our very prayers (as, indeed, he most plainly affirms in his writings) are of no other use, in his opinion, than to procure for us the explanation of the teaching by a divine revelation, not to procure help for the mind of man to perfect by love and action what it has learned should be done. The fact is, he does not in the least relinquish that very manifest dogma of his system in which he sets forth those three things, capacity, volition, action; maintaining that only the first of these, the capacity, is favored with the constant assistance of divine help, but supposing that the volition and the action stand in no need of God's assistance. Moreover, the very help which he says assists our natural capacity, he places in the law and teaching. This teaching, he allows, is revealed or explained to us by the Holy Ghost, on which account it is that he concedes the necessity of prayer. But still this assistance of law and teaching he supposes to have existed even in the days of the prophets; whereas the help of grace, which is properly so called, he will have to lie simply in the example of Christ. But this example, you can plainly see, pertains after all to "teaching,"—even that which is preached to us as the gospel. The general result, then, is the pointing out, as it were, of a road to us by which we are bound to walk, by the powers of our free will, and needing no assistance from anyone else, may suffice to ourselves not to faint or fail on the way. And even as to the discovery of the road itself, he contends that nature alone is competent for it; only the discovery will be more easily affected if grace renders assistance.

Chapter 46 [XLII]—Pelagius Professes to Respect the Catholic Authors.

Such are the particulars which, to the best of my ability, I have succeeded in obtaining from the writings of Pelagius, whenever he makes mention of grace. You perceive, however, that men who entertain such opinions as we have reviewed are "ignorant of God's righteousness, and desire to establish their own," and are far off from "the righteousness which we have of God" and not of ourselves; and this they ought to have discovered and recognized in the very holy canonical Scriptures. Forasmuch, however, as they read these Scriptures in a sense of their own, they of course fail to observe even the most obvious truths therein. Would that they would but turn their attention in no careless mood to what might be learned concerning the help of God's grace in the writings, at all events, of catholic authors; for they freely allow that the Scriptures were correctly understood by these, and that they would not pass them by in neglect, out of an overweening fondness for their own opinions. For note how this very man Pelagius, in that very treatise of his so recently put forth, and which he formally mentions in his self-defense (that is to say, in the third book of his Defense of Free Will), praises St. Ambrose.

Chapter 47 [XLIII.]—Ambrose Most Highly Praised by Pelagius.

"The blessed Bishop Ambrose," says he, "in whose writings the Roman faith shines forth with especial brightness, and whom the Latins have always regarded as the very flower and glory of their authors, and who has never found a foe bold enough to censure his faith or the purity of his understanding of the Scriptures." Observe the sort as well as the amount of the praises which he bestows; nevertheless, however holy and learned he is, he is not to be compared to the authority of the canonical Scripture. The reason of this high commendation of Ambrose lies in the circumstance, that Pelagius sees proper to quote a certain passage from his writings to prove that man can live without sin. This, however, is not the question before us. We are at present discussing that assistance of grace which helps us towards avoiding sin, and leading holy lives.

Chapter 48 [XLIV]. —Ambrose is Not in Agreement with Pelagius.

I wish, indeed, that he would listen to the venerable bishop when, in the second book of his Exposition of the Gospel according to Luke, he expressly teaches us that the Lord co-operates also with our wills. "You see, therefore," says he, "because the power of the Lord co-operates everywhere with human efforts, that no man is able to build without the Lord, no man to watch without the Lord, no man to undertake anything without the Lord. Whence the apostle thus enjoins: 'Whether ye eat, or whether ye drink, do all to the glory of God.'" You observe how the holy Ambrose takes away from men even their familiar expressions, —such as, "We undertake, but God accomplishes,"—when he says here that "no man is able to undertake anything without the Lord." To the same effect he says, in the sixth book of the same work, treating of the two debtors of a certain creditor: "According to men's opinions, he perhaps is the greater offender who owed most. The case, however, is altered by the Lord's mercy, so that he loves the most who owes the most, if he yet obtains grace." See how the catholic doctor most plainly declares that the very love which prompts every man to an ampler love appertains to the kindly gift of grace.

Chapter 49 [XLV.]—Ambrose Teaches with What Eye Christ Turned and Looked Upon Peter.

That repentance, indeed, itself, which beyond all doubt is an action of the will, is wrought into action by the mercy and help of the Lord, is asserted by the blessed Ambrose in the following passage in the ninth book of the same work: "Good, says he, "are the tears which wash away sin. They upon whom the Lord at last turns and looks, bewail. Peter denied Him first, and did not weep, because the Lord had not turned and looked upon him. He denied Him a second time, and still wept not, because the Lord had not even yet turned and looked upon him. The third time also he denied Him, Jesus turned and looked, and then he wept most bitterly." Let these persons read the Gospel; let them consider how that the Lord Jesus was at that moment within, having a hearing before the chief of the priests; whilst the Apostle Peter was outside, and down in the hall, sitting at one time with the servants at the fire, at another time standing, as the most accurate and consistent narrative of the evangelists shows. It cannot therefore be said that it was with His bodily eyes that the Lord turned and looked upon him by a visible and apparent admonition. That, then, which is described in the words, "The Lord turned and looked upon Peter," was affected internally; it was wrought in the mind, wrought in the will. In mercy the Lord silently and secretly approached, touched the heart, recalled the memory of the past, with His own internal grace visited Peter, stirred and brought out into external tears the feelings of his inner man. Behold in what manner God is present with His help to our wills and actions; behold how "He worketh in us both to will and to do."

Chapter 50. —Ambrose Teaches that All Men Need God's Help.

In the same book the same St. Ambrose says again: "Now if Peter fell, who said, 'Though all men shall be offended, yet will I never be offended,' who else shall rightly presume concerning himself? David, indeed, because he had said, 'In my prosperity I said, I shall never be moved,' confesses how injurious his confidence had proved to himself: 'Thou didst turn away Thy face,' he says, 'and I was troubled.'" Pelagius ought to listen to the teaching of so eminent a man, and should follow his faith, since he has commended his teaching and faith. Let him listen humbly; let him follow with fidelity; let him indulge no longer in obstinate presumption, lest he perish. Why does Pelagius choose to be sunk in that sea whence Peter was rescued by the Rock?

Chapter 51 [XLVI.]—Ambrose Teaches that It is God that Does for Man What Pelagius Attributes to Free Will.

Let him lend an ear also to the same godly bishop, who says, in the sixth book of this same book: "The reason why they would not receive Him is mentioned by the evangelist himself in these words, 'Because His face was as though He would go to Jerusalem.' But His disciples had a strong wish that He should be received into the Samaritan town. God, however, calls whomsoever He deigns, and whom He wills He makes religious." What wise insight of the man of God, drawn from the very fountain of God's grace! "God," says he, "calls whomsoever He deigns, and whom He wills He makes religious." See whether this is not the prophet's own declaration: "I will have mercy on whom I will have mercy, and will show pity on whom I will be pitiful;" and the apostle's deduction therefrom: "So then," says he, "it is not of him that wills, nor of him that runs, but of God that shows mercy." Now, when even his model man of our own times says, that "whomsoever God deigns He calls, and whom He wills He makes religious," will anyone be bold enough to contend that that man is not yet religious "who hastens to the Lord, and desires to be directed by Him, and makes his own will depend upon God's; who, moreover, cleaves so closely to the Lord, that he becomes (as the apostle says) 'one spirit' with Him?" Great, however, as is this entire work of a "religious man," Pelagius maintains that "it is effected only by the freedom of the will." But his own blessed Ambrose, whom he so highly commends in word, is against him, saying, "The Lord God calls whomsoever He deigns, and whom He wills He makes religious." It is God, then, who makes religious whomsoever He pleases, in order that he may "hasten to the Lord, and desire to be directed by Him, and make his own will depend upon God's, and cleave so closely to the Lord as to become (as the apostle says) 'one spirit' with Him;" and all this none but a religious man does. Who, then, ever does so much, unless he be made by God to do it?

Chapter 52 [XLVII.]—If Pelagius Agrees with Ambrose, Augustin Has No Controversy with Him.

Inasmuch, however, as the discussion about free will and God's grace has such difficulty in its distinctions, that when free will is maintained, God's grace is apparently denied; whilst when God's grace is asserted, free will is supposed to be done away with,—Pelagius can so involve himself in the shades of this obscurity as to profess agreement with all that we have quoted from St. Ambrose, and declare that such is, and always has been, his opinion also; and endeavor so to explain each, that men may suppose his opinion, to be in fair accord with Ambrose's. So far therefore, as concerns the questions of God's help and grace, you are requested to observe the three things which he has distinguished so very plainly, under the terms "ability," "will," and "actuality," that is, "capacity," "volition," and "action." If, then, he has come round to an agreement with us, then not the "capacity" alone in man, even if he neither wills nor performs the good, but the volition and the action also,—in other words, our willing well and doing well,—things which have no existence in man, except when he has a good will and acts rightly:—if, I repeat, he thus consents to hold with us that even the volition and the action are assisted by God, and so assisted that we can neither will nor do any good thing without such help; if, too, he believes that this is that very grace of God through our Lord Jesus Christ which makes us righteous through His righteousness, and not our own, so that our true righteousness is that which we have of Him,—then, so far as I can judge, there will remain no further controversy between us concerning the assistance we have from the grace of God.

Chapter 53 [XLVIII.]—In What Sense Some Men May Be Said to Live Without Sin in the Present Life.

But about the particular point in which he quoted the holy Ambrose with so much approbation, —because he found in that author's writings, from the praises he accorded to Zacharias and Elisabeth, the opinion that a man might possibly in this life be without sin; although this cannot be denied if God wills it, with whom all things are possible, yet he ought to consider more carefully in what sense this was said. Now, so far as I can see, this statement was made in accordance with a certain standard of conduct, which is among men held to be worthy of approval and praise, and which no human being could justly call in question for the purpose of laying accusation or censure. Such a standard Zacharias and his wife Elisabeth are said to have maintained in the sight of God, for no other reason than that they, by walking therein, never deceived people by any dissimulation; but as they in their sincerity appeared to men, so were they known in the sight of God. The statement, however, was not made with any reference to that perfect state of righteousness in which we shall one day live truly and absolutely in a condition of spotless purity. The Apostle Paul, indeed, has told us that he was "blameless, as touching the righteousness which is of the law;" and it was in respect of the same law that Zacharias also lived a blameless life. This righteousness, however, the apostle counted as "dung" and "loss," in comparison with the righteousness which is the object of our hope, and which we ought to "hunger and thirst after," in order that hereafter we may be satisfied with the vision thereof, enjoying it now by faith, so long as "the just do live by faith."

Chapter 54 [XLIX.]—Ambrose Teaches that No One is Sinless in This World.

Lastly, let him give good heed to his venerable bishop, when he is expounding the Prophet Isaiah, and says that "no man in this world can be without sin." Now nobody can pretend to say that by the phrase "in this world" he simply meant, in the love of this world. For he was speaking of the apostle, who said, "Our conversation is in heaven;" and while unfolding the sense of these words, the eminent bishop expressed himself thus: "Now the apostle says that many men, even while living in the present world, are perfect with themselves, who could not possibly be deemed perfect, if one looks at true perfection. For he says himself: 'We now see through a glass, darkly; but then face to face: now I know in part; but then shall I know, even as also I am known.' Thus, there are those who are spotless in this world, there are those who will be spotless in the kingdom of God; although, of course, if you sift the thing minutely, no one could be spotless, because no one is without sin." That passage, then, of the holy Ambrose, which Pelagius applies in support of his own opinion, was either written in a qualified sense, probable, indeed, but not expressed with minute accuracy; or if the holy and lowly-minded author did think that Zacharias and Elisabeth lived according to the highest and absolutely perfect righteousness, which was incapable of increase or addition, he certainly corrected his opinion on a minuter examination of it.

Chapter 55 [L.]—Ambrose Witnesses that Perfect Purity is Impossible to Human Nature.

He ought, moreover, carefully to note that, in the very same context from which he quoted that passage of Ambrose's, which seemed so satisfactory for his purpose, he also said this: "To be spotless from the beginning is an impossibility to human nature." In this sentence the venerable Ambrose does undoubtedly predicate feebleness and infirmity of that natural "capacity," which Pelagius refuses faithfully to regard as corrupted by sin, and therefore boastfully extols. Beyond question, this runs counter to this man's will and inclination, although it does not contravene the truthful confession of the apostle, wherein he says: "We too were once by nature the children of wrath, even as others." For through the sin of the first man, which came from his free will, our nature became corrupted and ruined; and nothing but God's grace alone, through Him who is the Mediator between God and men, and our Almighty Physician, succors it. Now, since we have already prolonged this work too far in treating of the assistance of the divine grace towards our justification, by which God co-operates in all things for good with those who love Him, and whom He first loved—giving to them that He might receive from them: we must commence another treatise, as the Lord shall enable us, on the subject of sin also, which by one man has entered into the world, along with death, and so has passed upon all men, setting forth as much as shall seem needful and sufficient, in opposition to those persons who have broken out into violent and open error, contrary to the truth here stated.

Book II.

On Original Sin.

Wherein Augustin shows that Pelagius really differs in no respect, on the question of original sin and the baptism of infants, from his follower Cœlestius, who, refusing to acknowledge original sin and even daring to deny the doctrine in public, was condemned in trials before the bishops—first at Carthage, and afterwards at Rome; for this question is not, as these heretics would have it, one wherein persons might err without danger to the faith. Their heresy, indeed, aimed at nothing else than the very foundations of Christian belief. He afterwards refutes all such as maintained that the blessing of matrimony is disparaged by the doctrine of original depravity, and an injury done to God himself, the Creator of man who is born by means of matrimony.

Chapter 1 [I.]—Caution Needed in Attending to Pelagius' Deliverances on Infant Baptism.

Next I beg of you, carefully to observe with what caution you ought to lend an ear, on the question of the baptism of infants, to men of this character, who dare not openly deny the laver of regeneration and the forgiveness of sins to this early age, for fear that Christian ears would not bear to listen to them; and who yet persist in holding and urging their opinion, that the carnal generation is not held guilty of man's first sin, although they seem to allow infants to be baptized for the remission of sins. You have, indeed, yourselves informed me in your letter, that you heard Pelagius say in your presence, reading out of that book of his which he declared that he had also sent to Rome, that they maintain that "infants ought to be baptized with the same formula of sacramental words as adults." Who, after that statement, would suppose that one ought to raise any question at all on this subject? Or if he did, to whom would he not seem to indulge a very calumnious disposition—before the perusal of their plain assertions, in which they deny that infants inherit original sin, and contend that all persons are born free from all corruption?

Chapter 2 [II.]—Cœlestius, on His Trial at Carthage, Refuses to Condemn His Error; The Written Statement Which He Gave to Zosimus.

Cœlestius, indeed, maintained this erroneous doctrine with less restraint. To such an extent did he push his freedom as actually to refuse, when on trial before the bishops at Carthage, to condemn those who say, "That

Adam's sin injured only Adam himself, and not the human race; and that infants at their birth are in the same state that Adam was in before his transgression." In the written statement, too, which he presented to the most blessed Pope Zosimus at Rome, he declared with especial plainness, "that original sin binds no single infant." Concerning the ecclesiastical proceedings at Carthage we copy the following account of his words.

Chapter 3 [III.]—Part of the Proceedings of the Council of Carthage Against Cœlestius.

"The bishop Aurelius said: 'Let what follows be recited.' It was accordingly recited, 'That the sin of Adam was injurious to him alone, and not to the human race.' Then, after the recital, Cœlestius said: 'I said that I was in doubt about the transmission of sin, but so as to yield assent to any man whom God has gifted with the grace of knowledge; for I have heard different opinions from those who have been even appointed presbyters in the Catholic Church.' The deacon Paulinus said: 'Tell us their names.' Cœlestius answered: 'The holy presbyter Rufinus, who lived at Rome with the holy Pammachius. I have heard him declare that there is no transmission of sin.' The deacon Paulinus then asked: 'Is there anyone else?' Cœlestius replied: 'I have heard more say the same.' The deacon Paulinus rejoined: 'Tell us their names.' Cœlestius said: 'Is not one priest enough for you?'" Then afterwards in another place we read: "The bishop Aurelius said: 'Let the rest of the accusation be read.' It then was recited 'That infants at their birth are in the same state that Adam was before the transgression;' and they read to the very end of the brief accusation which had been previously put in. [IV.] The bishop Aurelius inquired: 'Have you, Cœlestius, taught at any time, as the deacon Paulinus has stated, that infants are at their birth in the same state that Adam was before his transgression?' Cœlestius answered: 'Let him explain what he meant when he said, "before the transgression."' The deacon Paulinus then said: 'Do you on your side deny that you ever taught this doctrine? It must be one of two things: he must either say that he never so taught, or else he must now condemn the opinion.' Cœlestius rejoined: 'I have already said, Let him explain the words he mentioned, "before the transgression."' The deacon Paulinus then said: 'You must deny ever having taught this.' The bishop Aurelius said: 'I ask, What conclusion I have on my part to draw from this man's obstinacy; my affirmation is, that although Adam, as created in Paradise, is said to have been made immortal at first, he afterwards became corruptible through transgressing the commandment. Do you say this, brother Paulinus?' 'I do, my lord,' answered the deacon Paulinus. Then the bishop Aurelius said: 'As regards the condition of infants before baptism at the present day, the deacon Paulinus wishes to be informed whether it is such as Adam's was before the transgression; and whether it derives the guilt of transgression from the same origin of sin from which it is born?' The deacon Paulinus asked: 'Let him deny whether he taught this, or not.' Cœlestius answered: 'As touching the transmission of sin, I have already asserted, that I have heard many persons of acknowledged position in the catholic Church deny it altogether; and on the other hand, others affirm it: it may be fairly deemed a matter for inquiry, but not a heresy. I have always maintained that infants require baptism, and ought to be baptized. What else does he want?'"

Chapter 4. —Cœlestius Concedes Baptism for Infants, Without Affirming Original Sin.

You, of course, see that Cœlestius here conceded baptism for infants only in such a manner as to be unwilling to confess that the sin of the first man, which is washed away in the laver of regeneration, passes over to them, although at the same time he did not venture to deny this; and on account of this doubt he refused to condemn those who maintain "That Adam's sin injured only himself, and not the human race;" and "that infants at their birth are in the same condition wherein Adam was before the transgression."

Chapter 5 [V.]—Cœlestius' Book Which Was Produced in the Proceedings at Rome.

But in the book which he published at Rome, and produced in the proceedings before the church there, he so speaks on this question as to show that he really believes what he had professed to be in doubt about. For these are his words: "That infants, however, ought to be baptized for the remission of sins, according to the rule of the Church universal, and according to the meaning of the Gospel, we confess. For the Lord has determined that the kingdom of heaven should only be conferred on baptized persons; and since the resources of nature do not possess it, it must necessarily be conferred by the gift of grace." Now if he had not said anything elsewhere on this subject, who would not have supposed that he acknowledged the remission of original sin even in infants at their baptism, by saying that they ought to be baptized for the remission of sins? Hence the point of what you have stated in your letter, that Pelagius' answer to you was on this wise, "That infants are baptized with the same words of sacramental formula as adults," and that you were rejoiced to hear the very thing which you were desirous of hearing, and yet that you preferred holding a consultation with us concerning his words.

Chapter 6 [VI.]—Cœlestius the Disciple is In This Work Bolder Than His Master.

Carefully observe, then, what Cœlestius has advanced so very openly, and you will discover what amount of concealment Pelagius has practiced upon you. Cœlestius goes on to say as follows: "That infants, however, must be baptized for the remission of sins, was not admitted by us with the view of our seeming to affirm sin by transmission. This is very alien from the catholic meaning, because sin is not born with a man, —it is subsequently committed by the man for it is shown to be a fault, not of nature, but of the will. It is fitting, therefore, to confess this, lest we should seem to make different kinds of baptism; it is, moreover, necessary to lay down this preliminary safeguard, lest by the occasion of this mystery evil should, to the disparagement of the Creator, be said to be conveyed to man by nature, before that it has been committed by man." Now Pelagius was either afraid or ashamed to avow this to be his own opinion before you; although his disciple experienced neither a qualm nor a blush in openly professing it to be his, without any obscure subterfuges, in presence of the Apostolic See.

Chapter 7.—Pope Zosimus Kindly Excuses Him.

The bishop, however, who presides over this See, upon seeing him hurrying headlong in so great presumption like a madman, chose in his great compassion, with a view to the man's repentance, if it might be, rather to bind him tightly by eliciting from him answers to questions proposed by himself, than by the stroke of a severe condemnation to drive him over the precipice, down which he seemed to be even now ready to fall. I say advisedly, "down which he seemed to be ready to fall," rather than "over which he had actually fallen," because he had already in this same book of his forecast the subject with an intended reference to questions of this sort in the following words: "If it should so happen that any error of ignorance has stolen over us human beings, let it be corrected by your decisive sentence."

Chapter 8 [VII.]—Cœlestius Condemned by Zosimus.

The venerable Pope Zosimus, keeping in view this deprecatory preamble, dealt with the man, puffed up as he was with the blasts of false doctrine, so as that he should condemn all the objectionable points which had been alleged against him by the deacon Paulinus, and that he should yield his assent to the rescript of the Apostolic See which had been issued by his predecessor of sacred memory. The accused man, however, refused to condemn the objections raised by the deacon, yet he did not dare to hold out against the letter of the blessed Pope Innocent; indeed, he went so far as to "promise that he would condemn all the points which the Apostolic See condemned." Thus, the man was treated with gentle remedies, as a delirious patient who required rest; but, at the same time, he was not regarded as being yet ready to be released from the restraints of excommunication. The interval of two months being granted him, until communications could be received from Africa, a place for recovery was conceded to him, under the mild restorative of the sentence which had been pronounced. For in truth, if he would have laid aside his vain obstinacy, and be now willing to carry out what he had undertaken, and would carefully read the very letter to which he had replied by promising submission, he would yet come to a better mind. But after the rescripts were duly issued from the council of the African bishops, there were very good reasons why the sentence should be carried out against him, in strictest accordance with equity. What these reasons were you may read for yourselves, for we have sent you all the particulars.

Chapter 9 [VIII.]—Pelagius Deceived the Council in Palestine, But Was Unable to Deceive the Church at Rome.

Wherefore Pelagius, too, if he will only reflect candidly on his own position and writings, has no reason for saying that he ought not to have been banned with such a sentence. For although he deceived the council in Palestine, seemingly clearing himself before it, he entirely failed in imposing on the church at Rome (where, as you well know, he is by no means a stranger), although he went so far as to make the attempt, if he might somehow succeed. But, as I have just said, he entirely failed. For the most blessed Pope Zosimus recollected what his predecessor, who had set him so worthy an example, had thought of these very proceedings. Nor did he omit to observe what opinion was entertained about this man by the trusty Romans, whose faith deserved to be spoken of in the Lord, and whose consistent zeal in defense of catholic truth against this heresy he saw prevailing amongst them with warmth, and at the same time most perfect harmony. The man had lived among them for a long while, and his opinions could not escape their notice; moreover, they had so completely found out his disciple Cœlestius, as to be able at once to adduce the most trustworthy and irrefragable evidence on this subject. Now what was the solemn judgment which the holy Pope Innocent formed respecting the proceedings in the Synod of Palestine, by which Pelagius boasts of having been acquitted, you may indeed read in the letter which he addressed to me. It is duly mentioned also in the answer which was forwarded by the African Synod to the venerable Pope Zosimus and which, along with the other instructions, we have dispatched to your loving selves. But it seems to me, at the same time, that I ought not to omit producing the particulars in the present work.

Chapter 10 [IX.]—The Judgment of Innocent Respecting the Proceedings in Palestine.

Five bishops, then, of whom I was one, wrote him a letter, wherein we mentioned the proceedings in Palestine, of which the report had already reached us. We informed him that in the East, where this man lived, there had taken place certain ecclesiastical proceedings, in which he was thought to have been acquitted on all the charges. To this communication from us Innocent replied in a letter which contains the following among other words: "There are," says he, "sundry positions, as stated in these very Proceedings, which, when they were objected against him, he partly suppressed by avoiding them, and partly confused in absolute obscurity, by wresting the sense of many words; whilst there are other allegations which he cleared off,—not, indeed, in the honest way which he might seem at the time to use, but rather by methods of sophistry, meeting some of the objections with a flat denial, and tampering with others by a fallacious interpretation. Would, however, that he would even now adopt what is the far more desirable course of turning from his own error back to the true ways of catholic faith; that he would also, duly considering God's daily grace, and acknowledging the help thereof, be willing and desirous to appear, amidst the approbation of all men, to be truly corrected by the method of open conviction, —not, indeed, by judicial process, but by a hearty conversion to the catholic faith. We are therefore unable either to approve of or to blame their proceedings at that trial; for we cannot tell whether the proceedings were true, or even, if true, whether they do not really show that the man escaped by subterfuge, rather than that he cleared himself by entire truth." You see clearly from these words, how that the most blessed Pope Innocent without doubt speaks of this man as of one who was by no means unknown to him. You see what opinion he entertained about his acquittal. You see, moreover, what his successor the holy Pope Zosimus was bound to recollect, —as in truth he did, —so as to confirm without hesitation the judgment of his predecessor in this case.

Chapter 11 [X.]—How that Pelagius Deceived the Synod of Palestine.

Now I pray you carefully to observe by what evidence Pelagius is shown to have deceived his judges in Palestine, not to mention other points, on this very question of the baptism of infants, lest we should seem to anyone to have used calumny and suspicion, rather than to have ascertained the certain fact, when we alleged that Pelagius concealed the opinion which Cœlestius expressed with greater frankness, while at the same time he actually entertained the same views. Now, from what has been stated above, it has been clearly seen that Cœlestius refused to condemn the assertion that "Adam's sin injured only himself, and not the human race, and that infants at their birth are in the same state that Adam was before the transgression," because he saw that, if he condemned these propositions, he would affirm that there was in infants a transmission of sin from Adam. When, however, it was objected to Pelagius that he was of one mind with Cœlestius on this point, he condemned the words without hesitation. I am quite aware that you have read all this before. Since, however, we are not writing this account for you alone, we proceed to transcribe the very words of the synodal acts, lest the reader should be unwilling either to turn to the record for himself, or if he does not possess it, take the trouble to procure a copy. Here, then, are the words: —

Chapter 12 [XI.]—A Portion of the Proceedings of the Synod of Palestine in the Cause of Pelagius.

"The synod said: Now, forasmuch as Pelagius has pronounced his anathema on this uncertain utterance of folly, rightly replying that a man by God's help and grace is able to live ἀναμάρτητος, that is to say, without sin, let him give us his answer on other articles also. Another particular in the teaching of Cœlestius, disciple of Pelagius, selected from the heads which were mentioned and heard at Carthage before the holy Aurelius bishop of Carthage, and other bishops, was to this effect: 'That Adam was made mortal, and that he would have died, whether he sinned or did not sin; that Adam's sin injured himself alone, and not the human race; that the law no less than the gospel leads us to the kingdom; that before the coming of Christ there were persons without sin; that newborn infants are in the same condition that Adam was before the transgression; that, on the one hand, the entire human race does not die on account of Adam's death and transgression, nor, on the other hand, does the whole human race rise again through the resurrection of Christ; that the holy bishop Augustin wrote a book in answer to his followers in Sicily, on articles which were subjoined, and in this book, which was addressed to Hilary, are contained the following statements: That a man is able to be without sin if he wishes; that infants, even if they are unbaptized, have eternal life; that rich men, even if they are baptized, unless they renounce and give up all, have, whatever good they may seem to have done, nothing of it reckoned unto them, neither can they possess the kingdom of heaven.' Pelagius then said: As regards man's ability to be without sin, my opinion has been already spoken. With respect, however, to the allegation that there were even before the Lord's coming persons who lived without sin, we also on our part say, that before the coming of Christ there certainly were persons who passed their lives in holiness and righteousness, according to the accounts which have been handed down to us in the Holy Scriptures. As for the other points, indeed, even on their own showing, they are not of a character which obliges me to be answerable for them; but yet, for the satisfaction of the sacred Synod, I anathematize those who either now hold or have ever held these opinions."

Chapter 13 [XII.]—Cœlestius the Bolder Heretic; Pelagius the More Subtle.

You see, indeed, not to mention other points, how that Pelagius pronounced his anathema against those who hold that "Adam's sin injured only himself, and not the human race; and that infants are at their birth in the same condition in which Adam was before the transgression." Now what else could the bishops who sat in judgment on him have possibly understood him to mean by this, but that the sin of Adam is transmitted to infants? It was to avoid making such an admission that Cœlestius refused to condemn this statement, which this man on the contrary anathematized. If, therefore, I shall show that he did not really entertain any other opinion concerning infants than that they are born without any contagion of a single sin, what difference will there remain on this question between him and Cœlestius, except this, that the one is more open, the other more reserved; the one more pertinacious, the other more mendacious; or, at any rate, that the one is more candid, the other more astute? For, the one before the church of Carthage refused to condemn what he afterwards in the church at Rome publicly confessed to be a tenet of his own; at the same time professing himself "ready to submit to correction if an error had stolen over him, considering that he was but human;" whereas the other both condemned this dogma as being contrary to the truth lest he should himself be condemned by his catholic judges, and yet kept it in reserve for subsequent defense, so that either his condemnation was a lie, or his interpretation a trick.

Chapter 14 [XIII.]—He Shows That, Even After the Synod of Palestine, Pelagius Held the Same Opinions as Cœlestius on the Subject of Original Sin.

I see, however, that it may be most justly demanded of me, that I do not defer my promised demonstration, that he actually entertains the same views as Cœlestius. In the first book of his more recent work, written in defense of free will (which work he mentions in the letter he dispatched to Rome), he says: "Everything good, and everything evil, on account of which we are either laudable or blameworthy, is not born with us but done by us: for we are born not fully developed, but with a capacity for either conduct; and we are procreated as without virtue, so also without vice; and previous to the action of our own proper will, that alone is in man which God has formed." Now you perceive that in these words of Pelagius, the dogma of both these men is contained, that infants are born without the contagion of any sin from Adam. It is therefore not astonishing that Cœlestius refused to condemn such as say that Adam's sin injured only himself, and not the human race; and that infants are at their birth in the same state in which Adam was before the transgression. But it is very much to be wondered at, that Pelagius had the effrontery to anathematize these opinions. For if, as he alleges, "evil is not born with us, and we are procreated without fault, and the only thing in man before the action of his own will is what God has formed," then of course the sin of Adam did only injure himself, inasmuch as it did not pass on to his offspring. For there is not any sin which is not an evil; or a sin that is not a fault; or else sin was created by God. But he says: "Evil is not born with us, and we are procreated without fault; and the only thing in men at their birth is what God has formed." Now, since by this language he supposes it to be most true, that, according to the well-known sentence of his: "Adam's sin was injurious to himself alone, and not to the human race," why did Pelagius condemn this, if it were not for the purpose of deceiving his catholic judges? By parity of reasoning, it may also be argued: "If evil is not born with us, and if we are procreated without fault, and if the only thing found in man at the time of his birth is what God has formed," it follows beyond a doubt that "infants at their birth are in the same condition that Adam was before the transgression," in whom no evil or fault was inherent, and in whom that alone existed which God had formed. And yet Pelagius pronounced anathema on all those persons "who hold now, or have at any time held, that newborn babes are placed by their birth in the same state that Adam was in before the transgression,"—in other words, are without any evil, without any fault, having that only which God had formed. Now, why again did Pelagius condemn this tenet also, if it were not for the purpose of deceiving the catholic Synod, and saving himself from the condemnation of a heretical innovator?

Chapter 15 [XIV.]—Pelagius by His Mendacity and Deception Stole His Acquittal from the Synod in Palestine.

For my own part, however, I, as you are quite aware, and as I also stated in the book which I addressed to our venerable and aged Aurelius on the proceedings in Palestine, really felt glad that Pelagius in that answer of his had exhausted the whole of this question. To me, indeed, he seemed most plainly to have acknowledged that there is original sin in infants, by the anathema which he pronounced against those persons who supposed that by the sin of Adam only himself, and not the human race, was injured, and who entertained the opinion that infants are in the same state in which the first man was before the transgression. When, however, I had read his four books (from the first of which I copied the words which I have just now quoted), and discovered that he was still cherishing thoughts which were opposed to the catholic faith touching infants, I felt all the greater surprise at a mendacity which he so unblushingly maintained in a synod of the Church, and on so great a question. For if he had already written these books, how did he profess to anathematize those who had ever entertained the opinions alluded to? If he purposed, however, afterwards to publish such a work, how could he anathematize those who at the time were holding the opinions? Unless, to be sure, by some ridiculous subterfuge he meant to say that the objects of his anathema were such persons as had in some previous time held, or were then holding, these opinions;

but that in respect of the future—that is, as regarded those persons who were about to take up with such views—he felt that it would be impossible for him to prejudge either himself or other people, and that therefore he was guilty of no lie when he was afterwards detected in the maintenance of similar errors. This plea, however, he does not advance, not only because it is a ridiculous one, but because it cannot possibly be true; because in these very books of his he both argues against the transmission of sin from Adam to infants, and glories in the proceedings of the Synod in Palestine, where he was supposed to have sincerely anathematized such as hold the opinions in dispute, and where he, in fact, stole his acquittal by practicing deceit.

Chapter 16 [XV.]—Pelagius' Fraudulent and Crafty Excuses.

For what is the significance to the matter with which we now have to do of his answers to his followers, when he tells them that "the reason why he condemned the points which were objected against him, is because he himself maintains that primal sin was injurious not only to the first man, but to the whole human race, not by transmission, but by example;" in other words, not because those who have been propagated from him have derived any fault from him, but because all who afterwards have sinned, have imitated him who committed the first sin? Or when he says that "the reason why infants are not in the same state in which Adam was before the transgression, is because they are not yet able to receive the commandment, whereas he was able; and because they do not yet make use of that choice of a rational will which he certainly made use of, since otherwise no commandment would have been given to him"? How does such an exposition as this of the points alleged against him justify him in thinking that he rightly condemned the propositions, "Adam's sin injured only himself, and not the whole race of man;" and "infants at their birth are in the self-same state in which Adam was before he sinned;" and that by the said condemnation he is not guilty of deceit in holding such opinions as are found in his subsequent writings, how that "infants are born without any evil or fault, and that there is nothing in them but what God has formed,"—no wound, in short, inflicted by an enemy?

Chapter 17. —How Pelagius Deceived His Judges.

Now, is it by making such statements as these, meeting objections which are urged in one sense with explanations which are meant in another, that he designs to prove to us that he did not deceive those who sat in judgment on him? Then he utterly fails in his purpose. In proportion to the craftiness of his explanations, was the stealthiness with which he deceived them. For, just because they were catholic bishops, when they heard the man pouring out anathemas upon those who maintained that "Adam's sin was injurious to none but himself, and not to the human race," they understood him to assert nothing but what the catholic Church has been accustomed to declare, on the ground of which it truly baptizes infants for the remission of sins—not, indeed, sins which they have committed by imitation owing to the example of the first sinner, but sins which they have contracted by their very birth, owing to the corruption of their origin. When, again, they heard him anathematizing those who assert that "infants at their birth are in the same state in which Adam was before the transgression," they supposed him to refer to none others than those persons who "think that infants have derived no sin from Adam, and that they are accordingly in that state that he was in before his sin." For, of course, no other objection would be brought against him than that on which the question turned. When, therefore, he so explains the objection as to say that infants are not in the same state that Adam was in before he sinned, simply because they have not yet arrived at the same firmness of mind or body, not because of any propagated fault that has passed on to them, he must be answered thus: "When the objections were laid against you for condemnation, the catholic bishops did not understand them in this sense; therefore, when you condemned them, they believed that you were a catholic. That, accordingly, which they supposed you to maintain, deserved to be released from censure; but that which you really maintained was worthy of condemnation. It was not you, then, that were acquitted, who held tenets which ought to be condemned; but that opinion was freed from censure which you ought to have held and maintained. You could only be supposed to be acquitted by having been believed to entertain opinions worthy to be praised; for your judges could not suppose that you were concealing opinions which merited condemnation. Rightly have you been adjudged an accomplice of Cœlestius, in whose opinions you prove yourself to be a sharer. And though you kept your books shut during your trial, you published them to the world after it was over."

Chapter 18 [XVII.]—The Condemnation of Pelagius.

This being the case, you of course feel that episcopal councils, and the Apostolic See, and the whole Roman Church, and the Roman Empire itself, which by God's gracious favor has become Christian, has been most righteously moved against the authors of this wicked error, until they repent and escape from the snares of the devil. For who can tell whether God may not give them repentance to discover, and acknowledge, and even proclaim His truth, and to condemn their own damnable error? But whatever may be the bent of their own will, we cannot doubt that the merciful kindness of the Lord has sought the good of many persons who followed them, for no other reason than because they saw them associated in communion with the catholic Church.

Chapter 19. —Pelagius' Attempt to Deceive the Apostolic See; He Inverts the Bearings of the Controversy.

But I would have you carefully observe the way in which Pelagius endeavored by deception to overreach even the judgment of the bishop of the Apostolic See on this very question of the baptism of infants. He sent a letter to Rome to Pope Innocent of blessed memory; and when it found him not in the flesh, it was handed to the holy Pope Zosimus, and by him directed to us. In this letter he complains of being "defamed by certain persons for refusing the sacrament of baptism to infants, and promising the kingdom of heaven irrespective of Christ's redemption." The objections, however, are not urged against them in the manner he has stated. For they neither deny the sacrament of baptism to infants, nor do they promise the kingdom of heaven to any irrespective of the redemption of Christ. About, therefore, his complaint of being defamed by sundry persons, he has set it forth in such terms as to be able to give a ready answer to the alleged charge against him, without injury to his own dogma. [XVIII.] The real objection against them is, that they refuse to confess that unbaptized infants are liable to the condemnation of the first man, and that original sin has been transmitted to them and requires to be purged by regeneration; their contention being that infants must be baptized solely for being admitted into the kingdom of heaven, as if they could only have eternal death apart from the kingdom of heaven, who cannot have eternal life without partaking of the Lord's body and blood. This, I would have you know, is the real objection to them respecting the baptism of infants; and not as he has represented it, for the purpose of enabling himself to save his own dogmas while answering what is actually a proposition of his own, under color of meeting an objection.

Chapter 20. —Pelagius Provides a Refuge for His Falsehood in Ambiguous Subterfuges.

And then observe how he makes his answer, how he provides in the obscure mazes of his double sense retreats for his false doctrine, quenching the truth in his dark mist of error; so that even we, on our first perusal of his words, almost rejoiced at their propriety and correctness. But the fuller discussions in his books, in which he is generally forced, despite all his efforts at concealment, to explain his meaning, have made even his better statements suspicious to us, lest on a closer inspection of them we should detect them to be ambiguous. For, after saying that "he had never heard even an impious heretic say this" (namely, what he set forth as the objection) "about infants," he goes on to ask: "Who indeed is so unacquainted with Gospel lessons, as not only to attempt to make such an affirmation, but even to be able to lightly say it or even let it enter his thought? And then who is so impious as to wish to exclude infants from the kingdom of heaven, by forbidding them to be baptized and to be born again in Christ?"

Chapter 21 [XIX.]—Pelagius Avoids the Question as to Why Baptism is Necessary for Infants.

Now it is to no purpose that he says all this. He does not clear himself thereby. Not even they have ever denied the impossibility of infants entering the kingdom of heaven without baptism. But this is not the question; what we are discussing concerns the obliteration of original sin in infants. Let him clear himself on this point, since he refuses to acknowledge that there is anything in infants which the laver of regeneration has to cleanse. On this account we ought carefully to consider what he has afterwards to say. After adducing, then, the passage of the Gospel which declares that "whosoever is not born again of water and the Spirit cannot enter into the kingdom of heaven" (on which matter, as we have said, they raise no question), he goes on at once to ask: "Who indeed is so impious as to have the heart to refuse the common redemption of the human race to an infant of any age whatever?" But this is ambiguous language; for what redemption does he mean? Is it from evil to good? or from good to better? Now even Cœlestius, at Carthage, allowed a redemption for infants in his book; although, at the same time, he would not admit the transmission of sin to them from Adam.

Chapter 22 [XX.]—Another Instance of Pelagius' Ambiguity.

Then, again, observe what he subjoins to the last remark: "Can anyone," says he, "forbid a second birth to an eternal and certain life, to him who has been born to this present uncertain life?" In other words: "Who is so impious as to forbid his being born again to the life which is sure and eternal, who has been born to this life of uncertainty?" When we first read these words, we supposed that by the phrase "uncertain life" he meant to designate this present temporal life; although it appeared to us that he ought rather to have called it "mortal" than "uncertain," because it is brought to a close by certain death. But for all this, we thought that he had only shown a preference for calling this mortal life an uncertain one, because of the general view which men take that there is undoubtedly not a moment in our lives when we are free from this uncertainty. And so it happened that our anxiety about him was allayed to some extent by the following consideration, which rose almost to a proof, notwithstanding the fact of his unwillingness openly to confess that infants incur eternal death who depart this life without the sacrament of baptism. We argued: "If, as he seems to admit, eternal life can only accrue to them who have been baptized, it follows of course that they who die unbaptized incur everlasting death. This destiny, however, cannot by any means justly befall those who never in this life committed any sins of their own, unless on account of original sin."

Chapter 23 [XXI.]—What He Means by Our Birth to an "Uncertain" Life.

Certain brethren, however, afterwards failed not to remind us that Pelagius possibly expressed himself in this way, because on this question he is represented as having his answer ready for all inquirers, to this effect: "As for infants who die unbaptized, I know indeed whither they go not; yet whither they go, I know not;" that is, I know they do not go into the kingdom of heaven. But as to whether they go, he was (and for the matter of that, still is) in the habit of saying that he knew not, because he dared not say that those went to eternal death, who he was persuaded had never committed sin in this life, and whom he would not admit having inherited original sin. Consequently, those very words of his which were forwarded to Rome to secure his absolute acquittal, are so steeped in ambiguity that they afford a shelter for their doctrine, out of which may sally forth a heretical sense to entrap the unwary straggler; for when no one is at hand who can give the answer, any solitary man may find himself weak.

Chapter 24. —Pelagius' Long Residence at Rome.

The truth indeed is, that in the book of his faith which he sent to Rome with this very letter to the before-mentioned Pope Innocent, to whom also he had written the letter, he only the more evidently exposed himself by his efforts at concealment. He says: "We hold one baptism, which we say ought to be administered in the same sacramental words in the case of infants as in the case of adults." He did not, however, say, "in the same sacrament" (although if he had so said, there would still have been ambiguity), but "in the same sacramental words,"—as if remission of sins in infants were declared by the sound of the words, and not wrought by the effect of the acts. For the time, indeed, he seemed to say what was agreeable with the catholic faith; but he had it not in his power permanently to deceive that see. After the rescript of the African Council, into which province this pestilent doctrine had stealthily made its way—without, however, spreading widely or sinking deeply—other opinions also of this man were by the industry of some faithful brethren discovered and brought to light at Rome, where he had dwelt for a very long while, and had already engaged in sundry discourses and controversies. In order to procure the condemnation of these opinions, Pope Zosimus, as you may read, annexed them to his letter, which he wrote for publication throughout the catholic world. Among these statements, Pelagius, pretending to expound the Apostle Paul's Epistle to the Romans, argues in these words: "If Adam's sin injured those who have not sinned, then also Christ's righteousness profits those who do not believe." He says other things, too, of the same purport; but they have all been refuted and answered by me with the Lord's help in the books which I wrote, On the Baptism of Infants. But he had not the courage to make those objectionable statements in his own person in the fore-mentioned so-called exposition. This particular one, however, having been enunciated in a place where he was so well known, his words and their meaning could not be disguised. In those books, from the first of which I have already before quoted, he treats this point without any suppression of his views. With all the energy of which he is capable, he most plainly asserts that human nature in infants cannot in any wise be supposed to be corrupted by propagation; and by claiming salvation for them as their due, he does despite to the Savior.

Chapter 25 [XXII.]—The Condemnation of Pelagius and Cœlestius.

These things, then, being as I have stated them, it is now evident that there has arisen a deadly heresy, which, with the Lord's help, the Church by this time guards against more directly—now that those two men, Pelagius and Cœlestius, have been either offered repentance, or on their refusal been wholly condemned. They are reported, or perhaps actually proved, to be the authors of this perversion; at all events, if not the authors (as having learnt it from others), they are yet its boasted abettors and teachers, through whose agency the heresy has advanced and grown to a wider extent. This boast, too, is made even in their own statements and writings, and in unmistakable signs of reality, as well as in the fame which arises and grows out of all these circumstances. What, therefore, remains to be done? Must not every catholic, with all the energies wherewith the Lord endows him, confute this pestilential doctrine, and oppose it with all vigilance; so that whenever we contend for the truth, compelled to answer, but not fond of the contest, the untaught may be instructed, and that thus the Church may be benefited by that which the enemy devised for her destruction; in accordance with that word of the apostle's,

"There must be heresies, that they which are approved may be made manifest among you"?

Chapter 26 [XXIII.]—The Pelagians Maintain that Raising Questions About Original Sin Does Not Endanger the Faith.

Therefore, after the full discussion with which we have been able to rebut in writing this error of theirs, which is so inimical to the grace of God bestowed on small and great through our Lord Jesus Christ, it is now our duty to examine and explode that assertion of theirs, which in their desire to avoid the odious imputation of heresy they astutely advance, to the effect that "calling this subject into question produces no danger to the faith,"—in order that they may appear, forsooth, if they are convicted of having deviated from it, to have erred not criminally, but only, as it were, courteously. This, accordingly, is the language which Cœlestius used in the ecclesiastical process at Carthage: "As touching the transmission of sin," he said, "I have already said that I have heard many persons of acknowledged position in the catholic Church deny it, and on the other hand many affirm it; it may fairly, indeed, be deemed a matter for inquiry, but not a heresy. I have always maintained that infants require baptism, and ought to be baptized. What else does he want?" He said this, as if he wanted to intimate that only then could he be deemed chargeable with heresy, if he were to assert that they ought not to be baptized. As the case stood, however, inasmuch as he acknowledged that they ought to be baptized, he thought that he had not erred [criminally], and therefore ought not to be adjudged a heretic, even though he maintained the reason of their baptism to be other than the truth holds, or the faith claims as its own. On the same principle, in the book which he sent to Rome, he first explained his belief, so far as it suited his pleasure, from the Trinity of the One Godhead down to the kind of resurrection of the dead that is to be; on all which points, however, no one had ever questioned him, or been questioned by him. And when his discourse reached the question which was under consideration, he said: "If, indeed, any questions have arisen beyond the compass of the faith, on which there might be perhaps dissension on the part of a great many persons, in no case have I pretended to pronounce a decision on any dogma, as if I possessed a definitive authority in the matter myself; but whatever I have derived from the fountain of the prophets and the apostles, I have presented for approbation to the judgment of your apostolic office; so that if any error has crept in among us, human as we are, through our ignorance, it may be corrected by your sentence." You of course clearly see that in this action of his he used all this deprecatory preamble in order that, if he had been discovered to have erred at all, he might seem to have erred not on a matter of faith, but on questionable points outside the faith; wherein, however necessary it may be to correct the error, it is not corrected as a heresy; wherein also the person who undergoes the correction is declared indeed to be in error, but for all that is not adjudged a heretic.

Chapter 27 [XXIII.]—On Questions Outside the

Faith—What They Are, and Instances of the Same.

But he is greatly mistaken in this opinion. The questions which he supposes to be outside the faith are of a very different character from those in which, without any detriment to the faith whereby we are Christians, there exists either an ignorance of the real fact, and a consequent suspension of any fixed opinion, or else a conjectural view of the case, which, owing to the infirmity of human thought, issues in conceptions at variance with truth: as when a question arises about the description and locality of that Paradise where God placed man whom He formed out of the ground, without any disturbance, however, of the Christian belief that there undoubtedly is such a Paradise; or as when it is asked where Elijah is at the present moment, and where Enoch—whether in this Paradise or in some other place, although we doubt not of their existing still in the same bodies in which they were born; or as when one inquires whether it was in the body or out of the body that the apostle was caught up to the third heaven,—an inquiry, however, which betokens great lack of modesty on the part of those who would fain know what he who is the subject of the mystery itself expressly declares his ignorance of, without impairing his own belief of the fact; or as when the question is started, how many are those heavens, to the "third" of which he tells us that he was caught up; or whether the elements of this visible world are four or more; what it is which causes those eclipses of the sun or the moon which astronomers are in the habit of foretelling for certain appointed seasons; why, again, men of ancient times lived to the age which Holy Scripture assigns to them; and whether the period of their puberty, when they begat their first son, was postponed to an older age, proportioned to their longer life; or where Methuselah could possibly have lived, since he was not in the Ark, inasmuch as (according to the chronological notes of most copies of the Scripture, both Greek and Latin) he is found to have survived the deluge; or whether we must follow the order of the fewer copies—and they happen to be extremely few—which so arrange the years as to show that he died before the deluge. Now who does not feel, amidst the various and innumerable questions of this sort, which relate either to God's most hidden operations or to most obscure passages of the Scriptures, and which it is difficult to embrace and define in any certain way, that ignorance may on many points be compatible with sound Christian faith, and that occasionally erroneous opinion may be entertained without any room for the imputation of heretical doctrine?

Chapter 28 [XXIV.]—The Heresy of Pelagius and Cœlestius Aims at the Very Foundations of Our Faith.

This is, however, in the matter of the two men by one of whom we are sold under sin, by the other redeemed from sins—by the one have been precipitated into death, by the other are liberated unto life; the former of whom has ruined us in himself, by doing his own will instead of His who created him; the latter has saved us in Himself, by not doing His own will, but the will of Him who sent Him: and it is in what concerns these two men that the Christian faith properly consists. For "there is one God, and one Mediator between God and men, the man Christ Jesus;" since "there is none other name under heaven given to men, whereby we must be saved;" and "in Him hath God defined unto all men their faith, in that He hath raised Him from the dead." Now without this faith, that is to say, without a belief in the one Mediator between God and men, the man Christ Jesus; without faith, I say, in His resurrection by which God has given assurance to all men and which no man could of course truly believe were it not for His incarnation and death; without faith, therefore, in the incarnation and death and resurrection of Christ, the Christian verity unhesitatingly declares that the ancient saints could not possibly have been cleansed from sin so as to have become holy, and justified by the grace of God. And this is true both of the saints who are mentioned in Holy Scripture, and of those also who are not indeed mentioned therein, but must yet be supposed to have existed, —either before the deluge, or in the interval between that event and the giving of the law, or in the period of the law itself, —not merely among the children of Israel, as the prophets, but even outside that nation, as for instance Job. For it was by the self-same faith in the one Mediator that the hearts of these, too, were cleansed, and there also was "shed abroad in them the love of God by the Holy Ghost," "who blows where He lists," not following men's merits, but even producing these very merits Himself. For the grace of God will in no wise exist unless it be wholly free.

Chapter 29. —The Righteous Men Who Lived in

the Time of the Law Were for All that Not Under the Law, But Under Grace. The Grace of the New Testament Hidden Under the Old.

Death indeed reigned from Adam until Moses, because it was not possible even for the law given through Moses to overcome it: it was not given, in fact, as something able to give life; but as something that ought to show those that were dead and for whom grace was needed to give them life, that they were not only prostrated under the propagation and domination of sin, but also convicted by the additional guilt of breaking the law itself: not in order that any one might perish who in the mercy of God understood this even in that early age; but that, destined though he was to punishment, owing to the dominion of death, and manifested, too, as guilty through his own violation of the law, he might seek God's help, and so where sin abounded, grace might much more abound, even the grace which alone delivers from the body of this death. [XXV.] Yet, notwithstanding this, although not even the law which Moses gave was able to liberate any man from the dominion of death, there were even then, too, at the time of the law, men of God who were not living under the terror and conviction and punishment of the law, but under the delight and healing and liberation of grace. Some there were who said, "I was shapen in iniquity, and in sin did my mother conceive me;" and, "There is no rest in my bones, because of my sins;" and, "Create in me a clean heart, O God; and renew a right spirit in my inward parts;" and, "Stablish me with Thy directing Spirit;" and, "Take not Thy Holy Spirit from me." There were some, again, who said: "I believed, therefore have I spoken." For they too were cleansed with the self-same faith with which we ourselves are. Whence the apostle also says: "We having the same spirit of faith, according as it is written, I believe, and therefore have I spoken; we also believe, and therefore speak." Out of very faith was it said, "Behold, a virgin shall conceive and bear a son, and they shall call His name Emmanuel," "which is, being interpreted, God with us." Out of very faith too was it said concerning Him: "As a bridegroom He cometh out of His chamber; as a giant did He exult to run His course. His going forth is from the extremity of heaven, and His circuit runs to the other end of heaven; and no one is hidden from His heat." Out of very faith, again, was it said to Him: "Thy throne, O God, is for ever and ever; a scepter of righteousness is the scepter of Thy kingdom. Thou hast loved righteousness, and hated iniquity; therefore God, Thy God, hath anointed Thee with the oil of gladness above Thy fellows." By the self-same Spirit of faith were all these things foreseen by them as to happen, whereby they are believed by us as having happened. They, indeed, who were able in faithful love to foretell these things to us were not themselves partakers of them. The Apostle Peter says, "Why tempt ye God to put a yoke upon the neck of the disciples, which neither our fathers nor we were able to bear? But we believe that through the grace of the Lord Jesus Christ we shall be saved, even as they." Now on what principle does he make this statement, if it be not because even they were saved through the grace of the Lord Jesus Christ, and not the law of Moses, from which comes not the cure, but only the knowledge of sin? Now, however, the righteousness of God without the law is manifested, being witnessed by the law and the prophets. If, therefore, it is now manifested, it even then existed, but it was hidden.

This concealment was symbolized by the veil of the temple. When Christ was dying, this veil was rent asunder, to signify the full revelation of Him. Even of old, therefore there existed amongst the people of God this grace of the one Mediator between God and men, the man Christ Jesus; but like the rain in the fleece which God sets apart for His inheritance, not of debt, but of His own will, it was latently present, but is now patently visible amongst all nations as its "floor," the fleece being dry, — in other words, the Jewish people having become reprobate.

Chapter 30 [XXVI]—Pelagius and Cœlestius Deny that the Ancient Saints Were Saved by Christ.

We must not therefore divide the times, as Pelagius and his disciples do, who say that men first lived righteously by nature, then under the law, thirdly under grace, —by nature meaning all the long time from Adam before the giving of the law. "For then," say they, "the Creator was known by the guidance of reason; and the rule of living rightly was carried written in the hearts of men, not in the law of the letter, but of nature. But men's manners became corrupt; and then," they say, "when nature now tarnished began to be insufficient, the law was added to it whereby as by a moon the original luster was restored to nature after its blush was impaired. But after the habit of sinning had too much prevailed among men, and the law was unequal to the task of curing it, Christ came; and the Physician Himself, through His own self, and not through His disciples, brought relief to the malady at its most desperate development."

Chapter 31. —Christ's Incarnation Was of Avail to the Fathers, Even Though It Had Not Yet Happened.

By disputation of this sort, they attempt to exclude the ancient saints from the grace of the Mediator, as if the man Christ Jesus were not the Mediator between God and those men; because, not having yet taken flesh of the Virgin's womb, He was not yet man at the time when those righteous men lived. If this, however, were true, in vain would the apostle say: "By man came death, by man came also the resurrection of the dead; for as in Adam all die, even so in Christ shall all be made alive." For inasmuch as those ancient saints, according to the vain conceits of these men, found their nature self-sufficient, and required not the man Christ to be their Mediator to reconcile them to God, so neither shall they be made alive in Him, to whose body they are shown not to belong as members, according to the statement that it was on man's account that He became man. If, however, as the Truth says through His apostles, even as all die in Adam, even so shall all be made alive in Christ; forasmuch as the resurrection of the dead comes through the one man, even as death comes through the other man; what Christian man can be bold enough to doubt that even those righteous men who pleased God in the more remote periods of the human race are destined to attain to the resurrection of eternal life, and not eternal death, because they shall be made alive in Christ? that they are made alive in Christ, because they belong to the body of Christ? that they belong to the body of Christ, because Christ is the head even to them? and that Christ is the head even to them, because there is but one Mediator between God and men, the man Christ Jesus? But this He could not have been to them, unless through His grace they had believed in His resurrection. And how could they have done this, if they had been ignorant that He was to come in the flesh, and if they had not by this faith lived justly and piously? Now, if the incarnation of Christ could be of no concern to them, because it had not yet come about, it must follow that Christ's judgment can be of no concern to us, because it has not yet taken place. But if we shall stand at the right hand of Christ through our faith in His judgment, which has not yet transpired, but is to come to pass, it follows that those ancient saints are members of Christ through their faith in His resurrection, which had not in their day happened, but which was one day to come to pass.

Chapter 32 [XXVII.]—He Shows by the Example of Abraham that the Ancient Saints Believed in the Incarnation of Christ.

For it must not be supposed that those saints of old only profited by Christ's divinity, which was ever existent, and not also by the revelation of His humanity, which had not yet come to pass. What the Lord Jesus says, "Abraham desired to see my day, and he saw it, and was glad," meaning by the phrase his day to understand his time, affords of course a clear testimony that Abraham was fully imbued with belief in His incarnation. It is in respect of this that He has a "time;" for His divinity exceeds all time, for it was by it that all times were created. If, however, any one supposes that the phrase in question must be understood of that eternal "day" which is limited by no morrow, and preceded by no yesterday, —in a word, of the very eternity in which He is co-eternal with the Father, —how would Abraham really desire this, unless he was aware that there was to be a future mortality belonging to Him whose eternity he wished for? Or, perhaps, someone would confine the meaning of the phrase so far as to say, that nothing else is meant in the Lord's saying, "He desired to see my day," than "He desired to see me," who am the never-ending Day, or the unfailing Light, as when we mention the life of the Son, concerning which it is said in the Gospel: "So hath He given to the Son to have life in Himself." Here the life is nothing less than Himself. So we understand the Son Himself to be the life, when He said, "I am the way, the truth, and the life;" of whom also it was said, "He is the true God, and eternal life." Supposing, then, that Abraham desired to see this equal divinity of the Son's with the Father, without any precognition of His coming in the flesh—as certain philosophers sought Him, who knew nothing of His flesh—can that other act of Abraham, when he orders his servant to place his hand under his thigh, and to swear by the God of heaven, be rightly understood by anyone otherwise than as showing that Abraham well knew that the flesh in which the God of heaven was to come was the offspring of that very thigh?

Chapter 33 [XVIII.]—How Christ is Our Mediator.

Of this flesh and blood Melchizedek also, when he blessed Abram himself, gave the testimony which is very well known to Christian believers, so that long afterwards it was said to Christ in the Psalms: "Thou art a Priest forever, after the order of Melchizedek." This was not then an accomplished fact, but was still future; yet that faith of the fathers, which is the self-same faith as our own, used to chant it. Now, to all who find death in Adam, Christ is of this avail, that He is the Mediator for life. He is, however, not a Mediator, because He is equal with the Father; for in this respect He is Himself as far distant from us as the Father; and how can there be any medium where the distance is the very same? Therefore the apostle does not say, "There is one Mediator between God and men, even Jesus Christ;" but his words are, "The Man Christ Jesus." He is the Mediator, then, in that He is man, —inferior to the Father, by so much as He is nearer to ourselves, and superior to us, by so much as He is nearer to the Father. This is more openly expressed thus: "He is inferior to the Father, because in the form of a servant;" superior to us, because without spot of sin.

Chapter 34 [XXIX.]—No Man Ever Saved Save by Christ.

Now, whoever maintains that human nature at any period required not the second Adam for its physician, because it was not corrupted in the first Adam, is convicted as an enemy to the grace of God; not in a question where doubt or error might be compatible with soundness of belief, but in that very rule of faith which makes us Christians. How happens it, then, that the human nature, which first existed, is praised by these men as being so far less tainted with evil manners? How is it that they overlook the fact that men were even then sunk in so many intolerable sins, that, except for one man of God and his wife, and three sons and their wives, the whole world was in God's just judgment destroyed by the flood, even as the little land of Sodom was afterwards with fire? From the moment, then, when "by one man sin entered into the world, and death by sin, and so death passed upon all men, in whom all sinned," the entire mass of our nature was ruined beyond doubt, and fell into the possession of its destroyer. And from him no one—no, not one—has been delivered, or is being delivered, or ever will be delivered, except by the grace of the Redeemer.

Chapter 35 [XXX.]—Why the Circumcision of Infants Was Enjoined Under Pain of So Great a Punishment.

The Scripture does not inform us whether before Abraham's time righteous men or their children were marked by any bodily or visible sign. Abraham himself, indeed, received the sign of circumcision, a seal of the righteousness of faith. And he received it with this accompanying injunction: All the male infants of his household were from that very time to be circumcised, while fresh from their mother's womb, on the eighth day from their birth; so that even they who were not yet able with the heart to believe unto righteousness, should nevertheless receive the seal of the righteousness of faith. And this command was imposed with so fearful a sanction, that God said: "That soul shall be cut off from his people, whose flesh of his foreskin is not circumcised on the eighth day." If inquiry be made into the justice of so terrible a penalty, will not the entire argument of these men about free will, and the laudable soundness and purity of nature, however cleverly maintained, fall to pieces, struck down and fractured to atoms? For, pray tell me, what evil has an infant committed of his own will, that, for the negligence of another in not circumcising him, he himself must be condemned, and with so severe a condemnation, that that soul must be cut off from his people? It was not of any temporal death that this fear was inflicted, since of righteous persons, when they died, it used rather to be said, "And he was gathered unto his people;" or, "He was gathered to his fathers:" for no attempt to separate a man from his people is long formidable to him, when his own people is itself the people of God.

Chapter 36 [XXXI]—The Platonists' Opinion About the Existence of the Soul Previous to the Body Rejected.

What, then, is the purport of so severe a condemnation, when no willful sin has been committed? For it is not as certain Platonists have thought, because every such infant is thus requited in his soul for what it did of its own willfulness before the present life, as having possessed before its present bodily state a free choice of living either well or ill; since the Apostle Paul says most plainly, that before they were born they did neither good nor evil. On what account, therefore, is an infant rightly punished with such ruin, if it be not because he belongs to the mass of perdition, and is properly regarded as born of Adam, condemned under the bond of the ancient debt unless he has been released from the bond, not according to debt, but according to grace? And what grace but God's, through our Lord Jesus Christ? Now there was a forecast of His coming undoubtedly contained not only in other sacred institutions of the ancient Jews, but also in their circumcision of the foreskin. For the eighth day, in the recurrence of weeks, became the Lord's day, on which the Lord arose from the dead; and Christ was the rock whence was formed the stony blade for the circumcision; and the flesh of the foreskin was the body of sin.

Chapter 37 [XXXII.]—In What Sense Christ is Called "Sin."

There was a change of the sacramental ordinances made after the coming of Him whose advent they prefigured; but there was no change in the Mediator's help, who, even previous to His coming in the flesh, all along delivered the ancient members of His body by their faith in His incarnation; and in respect of ourselves too, though we were dead in sins and in the uncircumcision of our flesh, we are quickened together in Christ, in whom we are circumcised with the circumcision not made with the hand, but such as was prefigured by the old manual circumcision, that the body of sin might be done away which was born with us from Adam. The propagation of a condemned origin condemns us, unless we are cleansed by the likeness of sinful flesh, in which He was sent without sin, who nevertheless concerning sin condemned sin, having been made sin for us. Accordingly the apostle says: "We beseech you in Christ's stead, be ye reconciled unto God. For He hath made Him to be sin for us, who knew no sin; that we might be made the righteousness of God in Him." God, therefore, to whom we are reconciled, has made Him to be sin for us, —that is to say, a sacrifice by which our sins may be remitted; for by sins are designated the sacrifices for sins. And indeed He was sacrificed for our sins, the only one among men who had no sins, even as in those early times one was sought for among the flocks to prefigure the Faultless One who was to come to heal our offences. On whatever day, therefore, an infant may be baptized after his birth, he is as if circumcised on the eighth day; inasmuch as he is circumcised in Him who rose again the third day indeed after He was crucified, but the eighth according to the weeks. He is circumcised for the putting off of the body of sin; in other words, that the grace of spiritual regeneration may do away with the debt which the contagion of carnal generation contracted. "For no one is pure from uncleanness" (what uncleanness, pray, but that of sin?), "not even the infant, whose life is but that of a single day upon the earth."

Chapter 38 [XXXIII.]—Original Sin Does Not Render Marriage Evil.

But they argue thus, saying: "Is not, then, marriage an evil, and the man that is produced by marriage not God's work?" As if the good of the married life were that disease of concupiscence with which they who know not God love their wives—a course which the apostle forbids; and not rather that conjugal chastity, by which carnal lust is reduced to the good purposes of the appointed procreation of children. Or as if, forsooth, a man could possibly be anything but God's work, not only when born in wedlock, but even if he be produced in fornication or adultery. In the present inquiry, however, when the question is not for what a Creator is necessary, but for what a Savior, we have not to consider what good there is in the procreation of nature, but what evil there is in sin, whereby our nature has been certainly corrupted. No doubt the two are generated simultaneously—both nature and nature's corruption; one of which is good, the other evil. The one comes to us from the bounty of the Creator, the other is contracted from the condemnation of our origin; the one has its cause in the good-will of the Supreme God, the other in the depraved will of the first man; the one exhibits God as the maker of the creature, the other exhibits God as the punisher of disobedience: in short, the very same Christ was the maker of man for the creation of the one, and was made man for the healing of the other.

Chapter 39 [XXXIV.]—Three Things Good and Laudable in Matrimony.

Marriage, therefore, is a good in all the things which are proper to the married state. And these are three: it is the ordained means of procreation, it is the guarantee of chastity, it is the bond of union. In respect of its ordination for generation the Scripture says, "I will therefore that the younger women marry, bear children, guide the house;" as regards its guaranteeing chastity, it is said of it, "The wife hath not power of her own body, but the husband; and likewise also the husband hath not power of his own body, but the wife;" and considered as the bond of union: "What God hath joined together, let not man put asunder." Touching these points, we do not forget that we have treated at sufficient length, with whatever ability the Lord has given us, in other works of ours, which are not unknown to you. In relation to them all the Scripture has this general praise: "Marriage is honorable in all, and the bed undefiled." For, inasmuch as the wedded state is good, insomuch does it produce a very large amount of good in respect of the evil of concupiscence; for it is not lust, but reason, which makes a good use of concupiscence. Now lust lies in that law of the "disobedient" members which the apostle notes as "warring against the law of the mind;" whereas reason lies in that law of the wedded state which makes good use of concupiscence. If, however, it were impossible for any good to arise out of evil, God could not create man out of the embraces of adultery. As, therefore, the damnable evil of adultery, whenever man is born in it, is not chargeable on God, who certainly amidst man's evil work actually produces a good work; so, likewise, all which causes shame in that rebellion of the members which brought the accusing blush on those who after their sin covered these members with the fig-tree leaves, is not laid to the charge of marriage, by virtue of which the conjugal embrace is not only allowable, but is even useful and honorable; but it is imputable to the sin of that disobedience which was followed by the penalty of man's finding his own members emulating against himself that very disobedience which he had practiced against God. Then, abashed at their action, since they moved no more at the bidding of his rational will, but at their own arbitrary choice as it were, instigated by lust, he devised the covering which should conceal such of them as he judged to be worthy of shame. For man, as the handiwork of God, deserved not confusion of face; nor were the members which it seemed fit to the Creator to form and appoint by any means designed to bring the blush to the creature. Accordingly, that simple nudity was displeasing neither to God nor to man: there was nothing to be ashamed of, because nothing at first accrued which deserved punishment.

Chapter 40 [XXXV.]—Marriage Existed Before

Sin Was Committed. How God's Blessing Operated in Our First Parents.

There was, however, undoubtedly marriage, even when sin had no prior existence; and for no other reason was it that woman, and not a second man, was created as a help for the man. Moreover, those words of God, "Be fruitful and multiply," are not prophetic of sins to be condemned, but a benediction upon the fertility of marriage. For by these ineffable words of His, I mean by the divine methods which are inherent in the truth of His wisdom by which all things were made, God endowed the primeval pair with their seminal power. Suppose, however, that nature had not been dishonored by sin, God forbid that we should think that marriages in Paradise must have been such, that in them the procreative members would be excited by the mere ardor of lust, and not by the command of the will for producing offspring, —as the foot is for walking, the hand for labor, and the tongue for speech. Nor, as now happens, would the chastity of virginity be corrupted to the conception of offspring by the force of a turbid heat, but it would rather be submissive to the power of the gentlest love; and thus there would be no pain, no blood-effusion of the concumbent virgin, as there would also be no groan of the parturient mother. This, however, men refuse to believe, because it has not been verified in the actual condition of our mortal state. Nature, having been vitiated by sin, has never experienced an instance of that primeval purity. But we speak to faithful men, who have learnt to believe the inspired Scriptures, even though no examples are adduced of actual reality. For how could I now possibly prove that a man was made of the dust, without any parents, and a wife formed for him out of his own side? And yet faith takes on trust what the eye no longer discovers.

Chapter 41 [XXXVI.]—Lust and Travail Come from Sin. Whence Our Members Became a Cause of Shame.

Granted, therefore, that we have no means of showing both that the nuptial acts of that primeval marriage were quietly discharged, undisturbed by lustful passion, and that the motion of the organs of generation, like that of any other members of the body, was not instigated by the ardor of lust, but directed by the choice of the will (which would have continued such with marriage had not the disgrace of sin intervened); still, from all that is stated in the sacred Scriptures on divine authority, we have reasonable grounds for believing that such was the original condition of wedded life. Although, it is true, I am not told that the nuptial embrace was unattended with prurient desire; as also I do not find it on record that parturition was unaccompanied with groans and pain, or that actual birth led not to future death; yet, at the same time, if I follow the verity of the Holy Scriptures, the travail of the mother and the death of the human offspring would never have supervened if sin had not preceded. Nor would that have happened which abashed the man and woman when they covered their loins; because in the same sacred records it is expressly written that the sin was first committed, and then immediately followed this hiding of their shame. For unless some indelicacy of motion had announced to their eyes—which were of course not closed, though not open to this point, that is, not attentive—that those particular members should be corrected, they would not have perceived anything on their own persons, which God had entirely made worthy of all praise, that called for either shame or concealment. If, indeed, the sin had not first occurred which they had dared to commit in their disobedience, there would not have followed the disgrace which their shame would fain conceal.

Chapter 42 [XXXVII.]—The Evil of Lust Ought Not to Be Ascribed to Marriage. The Three Good Results of the Nuptial Ordinance: Offspring, Chastity, and the Sacramental Union.

It is then manifest that that must not be laid to the account of marriage, even in the absence of which, marriage would still have existed. The good of marriage is not taken away by the evil, although the evil is by marriage turned to a good use. Such, however, is the present condition of mortal men, that the connubial intercourse and lust are at the same time in action; and on this account it happens, that as the lust is blamed, so also the nuptial commerce, however lawful and honorable, is thought to be reprehensible by those persons who either are unwilling or unable to draw the distinction between them. They are, moreover, inattentive to that good of the nuptial state which is the glory of matrimony; I mean offspring, chastity, and the pledge. The evil, however, at which even marriage blushes for shame is not the fault of marriage, but of the lust of the flesh. Yet because without this evil it is impossible to affect the good purpose of marriage, even the procreation of children, whenever this process is approached, secrecy is sought, witnesses removed, and even the presence of the very children which happen to be born of the process is avoided as soon as they reach the age of observation. Thus, it comes to pass that marriage is permitted to affect all that is lawful in its state, only it must not forget to conceal all that is improper. Hence it follows that infants, although incapable of sinning, are yet not born without the contagion of sin, —not, indeed, because of what is lawful, but because that which is unseemly: for from what is lawful nature is born; from what is unseemly, sin. Of the nature so born, God is the Author, who created man, and who united male and female under the nuptial law; but of the sin the author is the subtlety of the devil who deceives, and the will of the man who consents.

Chapter 43 [XXXVIII.]—Human Offspring, Even Previous to Birth, Under Condemnation at the Very Root. Uses of Matrimony Undertaken for Mere Pleasure Not Without Venial Fault.

Where God did nothing else than by a just sentence to condemn the man who willfully sins, together with his stock; there also, as a matter of course, whatsoever was even not yet born is justly condemned in its sinful root. In this condemned stock carnal generation holds every man; and from it nothing but spiritual regeneration liberates him. In the case, therefore, of regenerate parents, if they continue in the same state of grace, it will undoubtedly work no injurious consequence, by reason of the remission of sins which has been bestowed upon them, unless they make a perverse use of it,—not alone all kinds of lawless corruptions, but even in the marriage state itself, whenever husband and wife toil at procreation, not from the desire of natural propagation of their species, but are mere slaves to the gratification of their lust out of very wantonness. As for the permission which the apostle gives to husbands and wives, "not to defraud one another, except with consent for a time, that they may have leisure for prayer," he concedes it by way of indulgent allowance, and not as a command; but this very form of the concession evidently implies some degree of fault. The connubial embrace, however, which marriage-contracts point to as intended for the procreation of children, considered in itself simply, and without any reference to fornication, is good and right; because, although it is by reason of this body of death (which is unrenewed as yet by the resurrection) impracticable without a certain amount of bestial motion, which puts human nature to the blush, yet the embrace is not after all a sin in itself, when reason applies the concupiscence to a good end, and is not overmastered to evil.

Chapter 44 [XXXIX.]—Even the Children of the Regenerate Born in Sin. The Effect of Baptism.

This concupiscence of the flesh would be prejudicial, just in so far as it is present in us, if the remission of sins were not so beneficial that while it is present in men, both as born and as born again, it may in the former be prejudicial as well as present, but in the latter present simply but never prejudicial. In the unregenerate it is prejudicial to such an extent indeed, that, unless they are born again, no advantage can accrue to them from being born of regenerate parents. The fault of our nature remains in our offspring so deeply impressed as to make it guilty, even when the guilt of the self-same fault has been washed away in the parent by the remission of sins—until every defect which ends in sin by the consent of the human will is consumed and done away in the last regeneration. This will be identical with that renovation of the very flesh itself which is promised in its future resurrection, when we shall not only commit no sins, but be even free from those corrupt desires which lead us to sin by yielding consent to them. To this blessed consummation advances are even now made by us, through the grace of that holy laver which we have put within our reach. The same regeneration which now renews our spirit, so that all our past sins are remitted, will by and by also operate, as might be expected, to the renewal to eternal life of that very flesh, by the resurrection of which to an incorruptible state the incentives of all sins will be purged out of our nature. But this salvation is as yet only accomplished in hope: it is not realized in fact; it is not in present possession, but it is looked forward to with patience. [XL.] And thus there is a whole and perfect cleansing, in the self-same baptismal laver, not only of all the sins remitted now in our baptism, which make us guilty owing to the consent we yield to wrong desires, and to the sinful acts in which they issue; but of these said wrong desires also, which, if not consented to by us, would contract no guilt of sin, and which, though not in this present life removed, will yet have no existence in the life beyond.

Chapter 45. —Man's Deliverance Suited to the Character of His Captivity.

The guilt, therefore, of that corruption of which we are speaking will remain in the carnal offspring of the regenerate, until in them also it be washed away in the laver of regeneration. A regenerate man does not regenerate, but generates, sons according to the flesh; and thus he transmits to his posterity, not the condition of the regenerated, but only of the generated. Therefore, be a man guilty of unbelief, or a perfect believer, he does not in either case beget faithful children, but sinners; in the same way that the seeds, not only of a wild olive, but also of a cultivated one, produce not cultivated olives, but wild ones. So, likewise, his first birth holds a man in that bondage from which nothing but his second birth delivers him. The devil holds him, Christ liberates him: Eve's deceiver holds him, Mary's Son frees him: he holds him, who approached the man through the woman; He frees him, who was born of a woman that never approached a man: he holds him, who injected into the woman the cause of lust; He liberates him, who without any lust was conceived in the woman. The former could hold all men in his grasp through one; nor does any deliver them out of his power but One, whom he was unable to grasp. The very sacraments indeed of the Church, which she administers with due ceremony, according to the authority of very ancient tradition (so that these men, notwithstanding their opinion that the sacraments are imitatively rather than really used in the case of infants, still do not venture to reject them with open disapproval),—the very sacraments, I say, of the holy Church show plainly enough that infants, even when fresh from the womb, are delivered from the bondage of the devil through the grace of Christ. For, to say nothing of the fact that they are baptized for the remission of sins by no fallacious, but by a true and faithful mystery, there is previously wrought on them the exorcism and the exsufflation of the hostile power, which they profess to renounce by the mouth of those who bring them to baptism. Now, by all these consecrated and evident signs of hidden realities, they are shown to pass from their worst oppressor to their most excellent Redeemer, who, by taking on Himself our infirmity in our behalf, has bound the strong man, that He may spoil his goods; seeing that the weakness of God is stronger, not only than men, but also than angels. While, therefore, God delivers small as well as great, He shows in both instances that the apostle spoke under the direction of the Truth. For it is not merely adults, but little babes too whom He rescues from the power of darkness, in order to transfer them to the kingdom of God's dear Son.

Chapter 46. —Difficulty of Believing Original Sin. Man's Vice is a Beast's Nature.

No one should feel surprise, and ask: "Why does God's goodness create anything for the devil's malignity to take possession of?" The truth is, God's gift is bestowed on the seminal elements of His creature with the same bounty wherewith "He makes His sun to rise on the evil and on the good, and sends rain on the just and on the unjust." It is with so large a bounty that God has blessed the very seeds, and by blessing has constituted them. Nor has this blessing been eliminated out of our excellent nature by a fault which puts us under condemnation. Owing, indeed, to God's justice, who punishes, this fatal flaw has so far prevailed, that men are born with the fault of original sin; but yet its influence has not extended so far as to stop the birth of men. Just so does it happen in persons of adult age: whatever sins they commit, do not eliminate his manhood from man; nay, God's work continues still good, however evil be the deeds of the impious. For although "man being placed in honor abided not; and being without understanding, is compared with the beasts, and is like them," yet the resemblance is not so absolute that he becomes a beast. There is a comparison, no doubt, between the two; but it is not because of nature, but through vice—not vice in the beast, but in nature. For so excellent is a man in comparison with a beast, that man's vice is beast's nature; still man's nature is never on this account changed into beast's nature. God, therefore, condemns man because of the fault wherewithal his nature is disgraced, and not because of his nature, which is not destroyed in consequence of its fault. Heaven forbid that we should think beasts are obnoxious to the sentence of condemnation! It is only proper that they should be free from our misery, inasmuch as they cannot partake of our blessedness. What, then, is there surprising or unjust in man's being subjected to an impure spirit—not because nature, but because that impurity of his which he has contracted in the stain of his birth, and which proceeds, not from the divine work, but from the will of man; — since also the impure spirit itself is a good thing considered as spirit, but evil in that it is impure? For the one is of God, and is His work, while the other emanates from man's own will. The stronger nature, therefore, that is, the angelic one, keeps the lower, or human, nature in subjection, because of the association of vice with the latter. Accordingly the Mediator, who was stronger than the angels, became weak for man's sake. So that the pride of the Destroyer is destroyed by the humility of the Redeemer; and he who makes his boast over the sons of men of his angelic strength, is vanquished by the Son of God in the human weakness which He assumed.

Chapter 47 [XLI.]—Sentences from Ambrose in Favor of Original Sin.

And now that we are about to bring this book to a conclusion, we think it proper to do on this subject of Original Sin what we did before in our treatise On Grace, —adduce in evidence against the injurious talk of these persons that servant of God, the Archbishop Ambrose, whose faith is proclaimed by Pelagius to be the most perfect among the writers of the Latin Church; for grace is more especially honored in doing away with original sin. In the work which the saintly Ambrose wrote, Concerning the Resurrection, he says: "I fell in Adam, in Adam was I expelled from Paradise, in Adam I died; and He does not recall me unless He has found me in Adam, —so as that, as I am obnoxious to the guilt of sin in him, and subject to death, I may be also justified in Christ." Then, again, writing against the Novatians, he says: "We men are all of us born in sin; our very origin is in sin; as you may read when David says, 'Behold, I was shapen in iniquity, and in sin did my mother conceive me.' Hence it is that Paul's flesh is 'a body of death;' even as he says himself, 'Who shall deliver me from the body of this death?' Christ's flesh, however, has condemned sin, which He experienced not by being born, and which by dying He crucified, that in our flesh there might be justification through grace, where previously there was impurity through sin." The same holy man also, in his Exposition of Isaiah, speaking of Christ, says: "Therefore as man He was tried in all things, and in the likeness of men He endured all things; but as born of the Spirit, He was free from sin. For every man is a liar, and no one but God alone is without sin. It is therefore an observed and settled fact, that no man born of a man and a woman, that is, by means of their bodily union, is seen to be free from sin. Whosoever, indeed, is free from sin, is free also from a conception and birth of this kind." Moreover, when expounding the Gospel according to Luke, he says: "It was no cohabitation with a husband which opened the secrets of the Virgin's womb; rather was it the Holy Ghost which infused immaculate seed into her unviolated womb. For the Lord Jesus alone of those who are born of woman is holy, inasmuch as He experienced not the contact of earthly corruption, because of the novelty of His immaculate birth; nay, He repelled it by His heavenly majesty."

Chapter 48. —Pelagius Rightly Condemned and Really Opposed by Ambrose.

These words, however, of the man of God are contradicted by Pelagius, notwithstanding all his commendation of his author, when he himself declares that "we are procreated, as without virtue, so without vice." What remains, then, but that Pelagius should condemn and renounce this error of his; or else be sorry that he has quoted Ambrose in the way he has? Inasmuch, however, as the blessed Ambrose, catholic bishop as he is, has expressed himself in the above-quoted passages in accordance with the catholic faith, it follows that Pelagius, along with his disciple Cœlestius, was justly condemned by the authority of the catholic Church for having turned aside from the true way of faith, since he repented not for having bestowed commendation on Ambrose, and for having at the same time entertained opinions in opposition to him. I know full well with what insatiable avidity you read whatever is written for edification and in confirmation of the faith; but yet, notwithstanding its utility as contributing to such an end, I must at last bring this treatise to a conclusion.

www.ingramcontent.com/pod-product-compliance
Lightning Source LLC
Chambersburg PA
CBHW052058070526
44584CB00017B/2244